OUT OF HER
MIND

OUT OF HER MIND

MIND

Women Writing on Madness

EDITED BY

REBECCA SHANNONHOUSE

THE MODERN LIBRARY

NEW YORK

2003 Modern Library Edition

Compilation copyright © 2000 by Random House, Inc.
Introduction and selection introductions copyright © 2000, 2003
by Rebecca Shannonhouse

Owing to limitations of space, permission acknowledgments
can be found on pages 193–95.

LIBRARY OF CONGRESS CATALOGING-IN-PUBLICATION DATA
Out of her mind: women writing on madness / edited by Rebecca Shannonhouse.—
p.   cm.
ISBN 0-375-75502-0 (pbk.)
1. Mental illness—Fiction. 2. Mentally ill women—Fiction. 3. American prose
literature—Women authors. 4. English prose literature—Women authors.
5. Mentally ill women—Biography. 6. Mentally ill, Writings of the. 7. Mental illness.
I. Shannonhouse, Rebecca.

PS648.M38 O98   2000
810.8'0353—dc21
99-042208

Modern Library website address: www.modernlibrary.com

A Wounded Deer—leaps highest—

—EMILY DICKINSON

ACKNOWLEDGMENTS

A number of people deserve credit for generously contributing, in various ways, to the completion of this anthology. I owe a tremendous debt of gratitude to my family, Shari Cartun, Sheila Anne Feeney, Marcie Cohn, Maureen Brady, Rebecca Day, Caledonia Kearns, Barbara Lounsberry, Nancy Milford, Evelyn Triantafillou, Ngaere Baxter, Sarah Andrews, Kathy Miles, Tracey Moore, Alice Berman, and Ray Caligiure. Another round of thanks goes to the Writers Room, the Woodstock Guild, Evelyn Somers of *The Missouri Review,* Mary Hussmann of *The Iowa Review,* Marlene Dube of *The Belletrist Review,* Sue Levy of the National Alliance for the Mentally Ill, and Perry Willett of the Victorian Women Writers Project.

I offer a special note of appreciation to the resourceful archivists and research professionals at the Interlibrary Loan Office of the Elmer Holmes Bobst Library at New York University, the New York Academy of Medicine, the Department of Rare Books and Special Collections at Princeton University, the Harry Ransom Humanities Research Center at the University of Texas at Austin, and the General Research Division of the New York Public Library's Humanities and Social Sciences Library. I am also indebted to Steven M. Cartun, M.D., Tamar P. Martin, Ph.D., and Peter Kroll, psychoanalyst, for their review of the clinical references that appear the introduction.

To the writers whose work appears here, to my editor Kate Niedzwiecki, who consistently offered impeccable counsel, and to my agent Sheree Bykofsky and her associate Janet Rosen, who supported this book throughout its development, I extend my thanks to all of you for bringing this collection to life.

And, finally, my eternal thanks to Maggie, whose loving spirit lives on.

Contents

INTRODUCTION

A century ago, in a genteel neighborhood of Montgomery, Alabama, a child was born who would eventually embody the freewheeling spirit of the 1920s flapper. Lavish and impulsive, Zelda Fitzgerald offered an alluring mix of privilege and melodrama to complement her young novelist husband, F. Scott Fitzgerald. The couple stormed through the New York and Paris party circuits, cutting a lasting image of beauty and flamboyance. He produced great works of literature; she wrote fiction and essays, painted, and dreamed of being a dancer. Before she turned thirty, however, Zelda's life would take an abrupt turn as she experienced the first of several mental breakdowns. To those who knew her, the great American flapper had slipped behind a veil of madness.

Like Zelda Fitzgerald, generations of other gifted, unconventional, and tormented women have seen their live   lipsed by mental illness. They have suffered from depression, sc   phrenia, manic depression, and other disorders. Their life ambitions have been derailed by illnesses that bring sadness, delusions, and fears—leaving one, as Zelda once described herself, "heart-broken, grief-stricken, spiritually sick."

Other talented, outlandish women have been labeled "mad" simply for defying societal norms. They are the ones, in the not too distant past, who were considered lunatics for rejecting their socially imposed roles as homemakers. They are the ones who were dragged to institutions for disagreeing with their husbands about religion. They are the ones, like Ann Hopkins, the seventeenth-century politician's wife, who, according to one observer, became insane after "giving herself wholly to reading and writing."

So what is "madness"? When is it mental illness? Or when is it the circumstances of a woman's life driving her "out of her mind"? These are the fundamental questions that first inspired this anthology. In looking for answers, my instincts guided me to literature and history. Ever since I first read about Zelda Fitzgerald some twenty years ago, her life has felt unresolved to me, like a stranded traveler in the back of my mind. Was she destined to be mentally ill, or was she overshadowed by her marriage, driven mad by her unfulfilled aspirations?

My purpose in creating this anthology was twofold: to compile selections from the writings of Zelda Fitzgerald and other twentieth-century women, such as Sylvia Plath, Susanna Kaysen, Kate Millett, and Lauren Slater, who have so deftly rendered their psychological turmoil in American literature; and to track down the other troubled, often misunderstood women whose forgotten writings on madness were buried, I suspected, somewhere on library shelves or confined to aging reels of microfilm.

At Princeton University, I read volumes of Zelda's manuscripts and letters, most of them composed in her brash, big-looped handwriting. While reviewing her lifetime of correspondence, I happened upon unpublished letters written during one of her many hospitalizations. Four of those letters are published here for the first time.

At other libraries, I began to unearth historical selections—many of them out of print—including an 1896 essay t l "The Confessions of a Nervous Woman"; an 1887 exposé des ng how the famed journalist Elizabeth Cochrane, better known as Nellie Bly, feigned insanity to investigate a mental institution; and an 1873 account by Elizabeth Parsons Ware Packard, whose husband had her committed after she publicly challenged his beliefs. For historical context, I turned to the reportage of another Victorian stalwart, the social reformer

Dorothea Dix, who, though she was not mad, single-handedly recounted the abuse of mentally ill women in several states.

During my searches, I came across other harrowing pieces of history. There were tales from the Middle Ages, detailing how those suffering from mental illness were considered lepers and sent away to remote countrysides or warehoused on a "Ship of Fools." Other stories spoke of public whippings and barred windows that allowed passersby to observe mad men and women shackled by chains. To represent this period, I have included an excerpt from *The Book of Margery Kempe*, which tells of the violent mental collapse of a medieval mystic.

Digging through old books and journals also confirmed the uniqueness of women's experiences in the world of mental illness. The notion of "hysteria," which some people once linked to witchcraft, had overtaken the public consciousness by the nineteenth century. With that came a preoccupation with the female reproductive system—the uterus, in particular, the Greek name for which gives us the word "hysteria"—which dictated many of the medical profession's misguided attempts to cure this broad, undefinable category of mental conditions. In the medical literature of the late 1800s, one can easily find references to gynecological procedures, such as removal of the ovaries or even cauterization of the clitoris, which doctors performed on their hysterical patients. Perhaps no other piece of writing embodies this era of oppression and medical injustice better than Charlotte Perkins Gilman's classic short story "The Yellow Wallpaper," which also is included in the collection.

Along the way, I read a great deal about the doctors who hoped to cure the so-called menace of hysteria. Yet I was struck by the icy tone of one in particular, Dr. Edward C. Mann, who in the 1880s wrote about hysteria in a medical journal: "T mental condition of a woman with hysteria is somewhat peculi , he explained. "The patient, when the hysterical feelings come upon her, does not feel disposed to make the slightest effort to resist them, and yields to her emotions, whatever may be. She will laugh or cry on the slightest provocation, and is very nervous and excitable. She cares nothing for her duties and seemingly takes pleasure in exaggerating all her slight discomforts and annoyances, and by her suspicious exacting and un-reasonable behavior makes life generally uncomfortable to those about her."

Perhaps no one professed to know more about unraveling mental chaos, though, than the Viennese neurologist who staked claim to the patient's unexplored dreams and fertile unconscious. Building from his studies of hysteria, Sigmund Freud introduced psychoanalysis at the turn of the century as a means of understanding neuroses. After implicating the lasting psychological impact of childhood traumas, he fathered the era of "talk therapy," which many authors have mined for its rich drama.

Throughout Sylvia Plath's devastating account of a doctor-patient therapeutic relationship in *The Bell Jar,* Dr. Mann's coarse statements about hysteria and Dr. Freud's theories of mental suffering seem to echo behind her prose. "I had imagined a kind, ugly, intuitive man looking up and saying 'Ah!' in an encouraging way, as if he could see something I couldn't, and then I would find words to tell him how I was so scared, as if I were being stuffed farther and farther into a black, airless sack with no way out," wrote Plath. "But Doctor Gordon wasn't like that at all. He was young and good-looking, and I could see right away he was conceited. . . . The whole time I was talking, Doctor Gordon bent his head as if he were praying, and the only noise apart from the dull, flat voice was the tap, tap, tap of Doctor Gordon's pen-cil at the same point on the green blotter, like a stalled walking stick."

Not long after patients were encouraged to talk about their mental distress, the medical establishment adopted more extreme measures, such as electroshock therapy (E.S.T.), insulin therapy, and the lobot-omy. For women whose mental illnesses defied medical doctrine, doc-tors increasingly prescribed massive surges of electrical currents delivered to the brain, large doses of insulin to ˙ ˙uce convulsions, or, for seemingly hopeless cases, a surgical operat :o sever nerve path-ways in the frontal lobes of the cerebrum. Mary Jane Ward's popular novel *The Snake Pit* and New Zealand writer Janet Frame's *Faces in the Water* are excerpted in this collection to portray the ominous world of E.S.T. during its early years of use.

The venue of such therapy was typically the dreaded asylum,

where generations of women have gained or lost their sanity, depending on one's viewpoint. At the urging of doctors, family members delivered the mentally ill to these austere institutions with the intention of rejuvenating the mind and spirits of those who could not find solace in their homes. Sadly, many asylums quickly gained a stronger reputation for the horror of their locked wards and punishing regimens than for the effectiveness of their institutional care. Like Zelda Fitzgerald's letters, *The Loony-Bin Trip* by Kate Millett captures the monotony and crushing isolation of day-to-day existence in a mental institution.

By the time I closed in on the latter part of the twentieth century, it was clear that mental illness had become inextricably tied to a vast array of prescription drugs. While some of these drugs are still delivered forcibly to women in institutions, others, such as Valium, Xanax, Paxil, and Prozac, to name just a few, are consumed eagerly by legions of devotees. To address some of the resulting philosophical questions about the influence of chemicals on one's true personality, the essays "Black Swans" by Lauren Slater and "Thorazine Shuffle" by the filmmaker Allie Light have been included in the collection.

Other questions—big, eternal ones about the meaning of insanity—appear as themes in many of the works excerpted here, such as the anonymously written *Autobiography of a Schizophrenic Girl* and *Girl, Interrupted* by Susanna Kaysen. In her memoir, Kaysen describes the onset of madness: "Experience is thick. Perceptions are thickened and dulled. Time is slow, dripping slowly through the clogged filter of thickened perception. The body temperature is low. The pulse is sluggish. The immune system is half-asleep. The organism is torpid and brackish. Even the reflexes are diminished, as if the lower leg couldn't be bothered to jerk itself out of its stupor when the knee is tapped."

The issue of family also asserts itself t   and time again in these writings. In contemporary stories and hist   :s alike, relatives exist as diminished, shattered figures beside the raging force of mania, despair, or paranoia. What are the experiences of those who cannot escape the heat of mental illness? What is the psychological toll of caring for someone who is emotionally troubled? *The Woman Warrior* by Maxine Hong Kingston and "Isolation" by Martha Ellen Hughes search for answers to these questions while also penetrating some of the family myths that shroud madness in so many cultures. In other excerpts, such as those from Signe Hammer's *By Her Own Hand* and Linda Gray Sexton's *Searching for Mercy Street,* the mother-daughter bond, and its attendant conflicts, is seen through the prism of suicide. As the newest addition to this collection, Maud Casey's essay "A Better Place to Live" beautifully illustrates how the calming presence of family members can help break the unwieldy force of mental illness.

In addition to the distinct psychiatric conditions, such as schizophrenia and obsessive-compulsive disorder, that are represented in the anthology, I felt that it was important to present a few selections about depression, the mental illness that affects nearly twice as many women as men. In the collection, excerpts from *The Beast* by Tracy Thompson and *Willow Weep for Me* by Meri Nana-Ama Danquah express the numbing sorrow and emptiness of the disorder that both writers and clinicians refer to as the "common cold" of mental illness. In her memoir, Danquah wrote: "Depression offers layers, textures, noises. At times depression is as flimsy as a feather, barely penetrating the surface of my life, hovering like a slight halo of pessimism. Other times it comes on gradually like a common cold or a storm, each day presenting new signals and symptoms until finally I am drowning in it. Most times, in its most superficial and seductive sense, it is rich and enticing. A field of velvet waiting to embrace me. It is loud and dizzying, inviting the tenors and screeching sopranos of thoughts, unrelenting sadness, and the sense of impending doom."

Though many of the writers whose work is included here have been widely read, their nonfictional and fictional accounts of mental illness have not been collected in a single volume. The scholar Roy Porter has written extensively about the history of madness in a number of books, including *The Greatest Benefit to M   ind* and *A Social History of Madness. The Female Malady* by Elai   Showalter and *The Madwoman in the Attic* by Sandra M. Gilbert and Susan Gubar also have been recognized as important studies. The institutionalization of women has been documented in Dr. Jeffrey L. Geller and psychologist Maxine Harris's wonderful collection *Women of the Asylum.* And feminist psychologist Phyllis Chesler has eloquently indicted the oppressive clinical tradition that has prevailed for so many years in her classic, *Women and Madness.* Yet the general topic of madness in women has not been addressed in a literary and historical collection, only in individual novels, essays, memoirs, and articles. With this anthology, I hope to create a collective voice that will speak for the mentally ill women who have so frequently been cast aside for their "otherness."

In researching this book, I also encountered a number of delightful women whose circumstances surrounding their madness were more remarkable than their writings. I have not included their work in the collection but offer two such remarkable stories here:

In 1890, a brazen 41-year-old known as Andrew M. Sheffield, who cursed and defied the conventions of feminine propriety, was committed to an Alabama mental asylum. An addict and an alleged arsonist who had an affair with a man who supplied her with drugs, she corresponded with a succession of governors in hopes of being moved to a prison. For thirty years, she was unsuccessful in her efforts and eventually died at the hospital. Her correspondence is published in *The Letters of a Victorian Madwoman,* edited by John S. Hughes.

Another Victorian eccentric was an Englishwoman named Georgina Weldon, whose husband tried to have her committed after learning that she believed her dead mother had been reincarnated as a pet rabbit, a claim that these days might win her a lucrative book contract and a place on the bestseller lists. However, by locking herself in the house and disguising herself as a nun so she could safely leave the premises, Weldon escaped from an alienist who had been instructed to escort her to an asylum. Her experiences eventually played a part in the reform of insanity laws, and in 1878 she published *The History of my Orphanage or the Outpourings of an Alleged Lunatic.*

In 1999, well over a century after Weldon eluded the asylum, the White House sponsored its first-ever conf   ice on mental health. At that gathering, mental illness was referrec   as the "last great stigma of the twentieth century." As we begin the twenty-first century, it is debatable how far society has advanced in its treatment of those who, seemingly at random, have been besieged by madness. Still, it is clear that there is an important body of literature that can reveal to others the largely private world of emotional suffering. The writers whose

works are collected in this anthology not only represent creative, ro-
manticized women, like Zelda Fitzgerald, Sylvia Plath, and so many
others, but also, in a sense, the silent, anonymous ones who, for generations, have existed behind harsh, impersonal statistics of mental illness. It is my hope that, with this book, their stories will also be told.

———

EDITOR'S NOTE: In the historical selections, some archaic spelling and
punctuation has been retained to reflect the stylistic conventions of
the era in which the piece was written. Also, Martha Ellen Hughes has
changed the names in her essay, "Isolation," to protect the privacy of
the individuals.

OUT OF HER
MIND

from

THE BOOK OF MARGERY KEMPE

MARGERY KEMPE

1436

An eccentric medieval mystic, Margery Kempe provides one of the earliest records of madness in women. Kempe was the daughter of an English mayor. She married at age twenty and gave birth to fourteen children. In addition to her role as a housewife, Kempe, who was known for her attachment to fine clothing, operated a brewery and a mill for a short time. After giving birth to a child, going "out of her mind"—as she phrased it—and losing her businesses, she eventually devoted her life to religion. In this excerpt, Kempe vividly describes her violent descent into madness as well as the breakdown of a woman she later visits. Undoubtedly illiterate, Kempe dictated the work to two scribes in 1436, referring to herself as "this creature." The Book of Margery Kempe *is believed to be the earliest autobiography written in English. It was first published in 1936.*

When this creature was twenty years of age, or somewhat more, she was married to a worshipful burgess [of Lynn] and was with child within a short time, as nature would have it. And after she had conceived, she was troubled with severe attacks of sickness until the child was born. And then, what with the labour pains she had in childbirth and the sickness that had gone before, she despaired of her life, believing she might not live. Then she sent for her confessor, for she had a thing on her conscience which she had never revealed before that time in all her life. For she was continually hindered by her enemy—the devil—always saying to her while she was in good health that she didn't need to confess but to do penance by herself alone, and all should be forgiven, for God is merciful enough. And therefore this creature often did great penance in fasting on bread and water, and performed other acts of charity with devout prayers, but she would not reveal that one thing in confession.

And when she was at any time sick or troubled, the devil said in her mind that she should be damned, for she was not shriven of that fault. Therefore, after her child was born, and not believing she would live, she sent for her confessor, as said before, fully wishing to be shriven of her whole lifetime, as near as she could. And when she came to the point of saying that thing which she had so long concealed, her confessor was a little too hasty and began sharply to reprove her before she had fully said what she meant, and so she would say no more in spite of anything he might do. And soon after, because of the dread she had of damnation on the one hand, and his sharp reproving of her on the other, this creature went out of her mind and was amazingly disturbed and tormented with spirits for half a year, eight weeks and odd days.

And in this time she saw, as she thought, devils opening their mouths all alight with burning flames of fire, as if they would have swallowed her in, sometimes pawing at her, sometimes threatening her, sometimes pulling her and hauling her about both night and day during the said time. And also the devils called out to her with great threats, and bade her that she should forsake her Christian faith and belief, and deny her God, his mother, and all the saints in heaven, her good works and all good virtues, her father, her mother, and all her friends. And so she did. She slandered her husband, her friends, and her own self. She spoke many sharp and reproving words; she recognized no virtue nor goodness; she desired all wickedness; just as the spirits tempted he   say and do, so she said and did. She would have killed herself ma time as they stirred her to, and would have been damned with them in hell, and in witness of this she bit her own hand so violently that the mark could be seen for the rest of her life. And also she pitilessly tore the skin on her body near her heart with her nails, for she had no other implement, and she would have done something worse, except that she was tied up and forcibly restrained both day and night so that she could not do as she wanted.

And when she had long been troubled by these and many other temptations, so that people thought she should never have escaped from them alive, then one time as she lay by herself and her keepers were not with her, our merciful Lord Christ Jesus—ever to be trusted, worshipped be his name, never forsaking his servant in time of need—appeared to his creature who had forsaken him, in the likeness of a man, the most seemly, most beauteous, and most amiable that ever might be seen with man's eye, clad in a mantle of purple silk, sitting upon her bedside, looking upon her with so blessed a countenance that she was strengthened in all her spirits, and he said to her these words: "Daughter, why have you forsaken me, and I never forsook you?"

And as soon as he had said these words, she saw truly how the air opened as bright as any lightning, and he ascended up into the air, not hastily and quickly, but beautifully and gradually, so that she could clearly behold him in the air until it closed up again.

And presently the creature grew as calm in her wits and her reason as she ever was before, and asked her husband, as soon as he came to her, if she could have the keys of the buttery to get her food and drink as she had done before. Her maids and her keepers advised him that he should not deliver up any keys to her, for they said she would only give away such goods as there were, because she did not know what she was saying, as they believed.

Nevertheless, her husband, who always had tenderness and compassion for her, ordered that they should give her the keys. And she took food and drink as her bodily strength would allow her, and she once again recognized her friends and her household, and everybody else who came to her in order to see how r Lord Jesus Christ had worked his grace in her—blessed may he l , ho is ever near in tribulation. When people think he is far away from them he is very near through his grace. Afterwards this creature performed all her responsibilities wisely and soberly enough, except that she did not truly know our Lord's power to draw us to him. . . .

As the said creature was in a church of St. Margaret to say her devotions, there came a man and knelt behind her back, wringing his hands and showing signs of great distress. She, perceiving his distress, asked what was troubling him. He said things were very difficult for him, because his wife had just had a baby, and she was out of her mind.

"And, lady," he said, "she doesn't know me, or any of her neighbours. She roars and cries, so that she scares folk badly. She'll both hit out and bite, and so she's manacled on her wrists."

Then she asked the man if he would like her to go with him and see her, and he said, "Yes, lady, for God's love." So she went off with him to see the woman. And when she came into the house, as soon as that sick woman who had lost her reason saw her, she spoke to her seriously and kindly, and said she was most welcome to her. And she was very glad she had come, and greatly comforted by her presence. "For you are," she said, "a very good woman, and I behold many fair angels round about you, and therefore, I pray you, don't leave me, for I am greatly comforted by you."

And when other people came to her, she cried and gaped as if she would have eaten them, and said that she saw many devils around them. She would not willingly allow them to touch her. She roared and cried so, for the most part of both day and night, that people would not allow her to live amongst them, she was so tiresome to them. Then she was taken to a room at the furthest end of the town, so that people should not hear her crying. And there she was bound hand and foot with chains of iron, so that she should not strike anybody.

And the said creature went to her each day, once or twice at least; and while she was with her she was meek enough, and heard her talk and chat willingly, and without any roaring or crying. And the said creature prayed for this woman every day that ͞d should, if it were his will, restore her to her wits again. And ou ͗rd answered in her soul and said she should get on very well. Then she was bolder to pray for her recovery than she was before, and each day, weeping and sorrowing, prayed for her recovery until God gave her her wits and her mind again. And then she was brought to church and purified as other women are, blessed may God be.

It was, as they thought who knew about it, a very great miracle, for he who wrote this book had never before that time seen any man or woman, as he thought, so far out of herself as this woman was, nor so hard to control, and afterwards he saw her serious and sober enough—worship and praise be to our Lord without end for his high mercy and his goodness, who ever helps at time of need.

from

"ON BEHALF OF THE INSANE POOR"

DOROTHEA DIX

1843

As a nineteenth-century social reformer, Dorothea Dix visited prisons, almshouses, and insane asylums to report on the plight of mentally ill women and men. Dix was a former schoolteacher and children's book author and began her investigations after discovering that mental patients were housed at a prison where she led a Sunday school class. Her stark portraits of abuse ultimately led to the creation or expansion of dozens of mental hospitals in the United States and abroad. In this excerpt, Dix informs the Massachusetts legislature of the deplorable conditions women endured at institutions throughout the state. During the Civil War, Dix set aside her reform work to serve as Superintendent of Women Nurses in the Union army. Afterward, she resumed her campaign until retiring at age seventy-nine.

... I shall be obliged to speak with great plainness, and to reveal many things revolting to the taste, and from which my woman's nature shrinks with peculiar sensitiveness. But truth is the highest consideration. *I tell what I have seen*—painful and shocking as the details often are—that from them you may feel more deeply the imperative obligation which lies upon you to prevent the possi···· y of a repetition or continuance of such outrages upon humanit   I inflict pain upon you, and move you to horror, it is to acquaint you with sufferings which you have the power to alleviate, and make you hasten to the relief of the victims of legalized barbarity.

I come to present the strong claims of suffering humanity. I come to place before the Legislature of Massachusetts the condition of the miserable, the desolate, the outcast. I come as the advocate of helpless, forgotten, insane and idiotic men and women; of beings, sunk to a condition from which the most unconcerned would start with real horror; of beings wretched in our Prisons, and more wretched in our Alms-Houses. And I cannot suppose it needful to employ earnest persuasion, or stubborn argument, in order to arrest and fix attention upon a subject, only the more strongly pressing in its claims, because it is revolting and disgusting in its details.

I must confine myself to few examples, but am ready to furnish other and more complete details, if required. If my pictures are displeasing, coarse, and severe, my subjects, it must be recollected, offer no tranquil, refined, or composing features. The condition of human beings, reduced to the extremest states of degradation and misery, cannot be exhibited in softened language, or adorn a polished page.

I proceed, Gentlemen, briefly to call your attention to the *present* state of Insane Persons confined within this Commonwealth, in *cages, closets, cellars, stalls, pens! Chained, naked, beaten with rods,* and *lashed* into obedience!

As I state cold, severe *facts,* I feel obliged to refer to persons, and definitely to indicate localities. But it is upon my subject, not upon localities or individuals, I desire to fix attention; and I would speak as kindly as possible of all Wardens, Keepers, and other responsible officers, believing that *most* of these have erred not through hardness of heart and wilful cruelty, so much as want of skill and knowledge, and want of consideration. Familiarity with suffering, it is said, blunts the sensibilities, and where neglect once finds a footing other injuries are multiplied. This is not all, for it may justly and strongly be added that, from the deficiency of adequate means to meet the wants of these cases, it has been an absolute impossibility to do justice in this matter. Prisons are not constructed in view of be converted into County Hospitals, and Alms-Houses are not found is receptacles for the Insane. And yet, in the face of justice and common sense, Wardens are by law compelled to receive, and the Masters of Alms-Houses not to refuse, Insane and Idiotic subjects in all stages of mental disease and privation.

It is the Commonwealth, not its integral parts, that is accountable for most of the abuses which have lately, and do still exist. I repeat it, it is defective legislation which perpetuates and multiplies these abuses.

In illustration of my subject, I offer the following extracts from my Note-Book and Journal:—

Springfield. In the jail, one lunatic woman, furiously mad, a state pauper, improperly situated, both in regard to the prisoners, the keepers, and herself. It is a case of extreme self-forgetfulness and oblivion to all the decencies of life; to describe which, would be to repeat only the grossest scenes. She is much worse since leaving Worcester. In the almshouse of the same town is a woman apparently only needing judicious care, and some well-chosen employment, to make it unnecessary to confine her in solitude, in a dreary unfurnished room. Her appeals for employment and companionship are most touching, but the mistress replied, "she had no time to attend to her. . . ."

Burlington. A woman, declared to be very insane; decent room and bed; but not allowed to rise oftener, the mistress said, "than every other day: it is too much trouble."

Concord. A woman from the hospital in a cage in the almshouse. In the jail several, decently cared for in general, but not properly placed in a prison. Violent, noisy, unmanageable most of the time. . . .

Brewster. One woman violently mad, solitary: could not see her, the master and mistress being absent, and the paupers in charge having strict orders to admit no one. . . .

Danvers. November; visited the almshouse; a large building, much out of repair; understand a new one is in contemplation. . . .

Long before reaching the house, wild shouts, snatches of rude songs, imprecations, and obscene language, fell upon the ear, proceeding from the occupant of a low building, rather remote from the principal building to which my course was directed. Found the mistress, and was conducted to the place, which was called "*the home*" of th   *lorn* maniac, a young woman, exhibiting a condition of neglect and misery blotting out the faintest idea of comfort, and outraging every sentiment of decency. She had been, I learnt, "a respectable person; industrious and worthy; disappointments and trials shook her mind, and finally laid prostrate reason and self-control; she became a maniac for life! She had been at Worcester Hospital for a considerable time, and had been returned as incurable." The mistress told me she understood that, while there, she was "comfortable and decent." Alas! what a change was here exhibited! She had passed from one degree of violence and degradation to another, in swift progress; there she stood, clinging to, or beating upon, the bars of her caged apartment, the contracted size of which afforded space only for increasing accumulations of filth, a *foul* spectacle; there she stood with naked arms and dishevelled hair; the unwashed frame invested with fragments of unclean garments, the air so extremely offensive, though ventilation was afforded on all sides save one, that it was not possible to remain beyond a few moments without retreating for recovery to the outward air. Irritation of body, produced by utter filth and exposure, incited her to the horrid process of tearing off her skin by inches; her face, neck, and person, were thus disfigured to hideousness; she held up a fragment just rent off; to my exclamation of horror, the mistress replied, "oh, we can't help it; half the skin is off sometimes; we can do nothing with her; and it makes no difference what she eats, for she consumes her own filth as readily as the food which is brought her. . . ."

Some may say these things cannot be remedied; these furious maniacs are not to be raised from these base conditions. I *know* they are; could give *many* examples; let *one* suffice. A young woman, a pauper, in a distant town, *Sandisfield,* was for years a raging maniac. A cage, chains, and *the whip,* were the agents for controlling her, united with harsh tones and profane language. Annually, with others (the town's poor) she was put up at auction, and bid off at the lowest price which was declared for her. One year, not long past, an old man came forward in the number of applicants for the poor wretch; he was taunted and ridiculed; "what would he and his old wife do with such a mere beast?" "My wife says yes," replied he, "and I shall take her." She was given to his charge; he conveyed her home; she was washed, neatly dressed, and placed in a decent bed-room, furnished for comfort and opening into the kitchen. How altered her condition! A t *the chains* were not off. The first week she was somewhat restless, at times violent, but the quiet kind ways of the old people wrought a change; she received her food decently; forsook acts of violence, and no longer uttered blasphemous or indecent language; after a week, the chain was lengthened, and she was received as a companion into the kitchen. Soon she engaged in trivial employments. "After a fortnight," said the old man, "I knocked off the chains and made her a free woman." She is at times excited, but not violently; they are careful of her diet; they keep her very clean; she calls them "father" and "mother." Go there now and you will find her "clothed," and though not perfectly in her "right mind," so far restored as to be a safe and comfortable inmate....

> *Saugus.* December 24; thermometer below zero; drove to the poorhouse.... Was led through an outer passage into a lower room, occupied by the paupers; crowded; not neat; ascended a rather low flight of stairs upon an open entry, through the floor of which was introduced a stove pipe, carried along a *few feet,* about six inches above the floor, through which it was reconveyed below. From this entry opens a room of moderate size, having a sashed-window; floor, I think, painted; apartment ENTIRELY unfurnished; no chair, table, nor bed; neither, what is seldom missing, a bundle of straw or lock of hay; cold, very cold; the first movement of my conductor was to throw open a window, a measure imperatively necessary for those who entered. *On the floor* sat a woman, her limbs immovably contracted, so that the knees were brought upward to the chin; the face was concealed; the head rested on the folded arms; for clothing she appeared to have been furnished with *fragments* of many discharged garments; these were folded about her, yet they little benefitted her, if one might judge by the constant shuddering which almost convulsed her poor crippled frame. Woful was this scene; language is feeble to record the misery she was suffering and had suffered! In reply to my inquiry if she could not change her position, I was answered by the master in the negative, and told that the contraction of limbs was occasioned by "neglect and exposure in former years," but *since she had been crazy,* and before she fell under the charge, as I inferred, of her present *guardians.* Poor wretch! she, like many others, was an example of what humanity becomes when the temple of reason falls in ruins, leaving the mortal part to injury and neglect, and showing how much can be endured of privation, exposure, and disease,   out extinguishing the lamp of life....

Violence and severity do but exasperate the Insane: the only availing influence is kindness and firmness. It is amazing what these will produce. How many examples might illustrate this position: I refer to one recently exhibited in Barre. The town Paupers are disposed of annually to some family who, for a stipulated sum agree to take charge of them. One of them, a young woman, was shown to me well clothed, neat, quiet, and employed at needle-work. Is it possible that this is the same being who, but last year, was a raving madwoman, exhibiting every degree of violence in action and speech; a very tigress wrought to fury; caged, chained, beaten, loaded with injuries, and exhibiting the passions which an iron rule might be expected to stimulate and sustain. It is the same person; another family hold her in charge who better understand human nature and human influences; she is no longer chained, caged, and beaten; but if excited, a pair of mittens drawn over the hands secures from mischief. Where will she be next year, after the annual sale? . . .

Westford. Not many miles distant from Wayland is a sad spectacle; was told by the family who kept the poorhouse, that they had twenty-six paupers; one idiot; one simple; and one insane, an incurable case from Worcester hospital. I requested to see her, but was answered that she "wasn't fit to be seen; she was naked, and made so much trouble they did not know how to get along." I hesitated but a moment; I must see her, I said. I cannot adopt descriptions of the condition of the insane secondarily; what I assert for fact, I must see for myself. On this I was conducted above stairs into an apartment of decent size, pleasant aspect from abroad, and tolerably comfortable in its general appearance; but the inmates!—grant I may never look upon another such scene! A young woman, whose person was partially covered with portions of a blanket, sat upon the floor; her hair dishevelled; her naked arms crossed languidly over the breast; a distracted, unsteady eye, and low, murmuring voice, betraying both mental and physical disquiet. *About the waist was a chain,* the extremity of which was fastened into the wall of the house. As I entered she raised her eyes, blushed, moved uneasily, endeavoring at the same time to draw about her the insufficient fragments of the blanket. I knelt beside her and asked if she did not wish to be dressed? "Yes; I want some c   es." "But you'll tear 'em all up, you know you will," interposed her attendant. "No, I won't, I won't tear them off;" and she tried to rise, but the waist-encircling chain threw her back, and she did not renew the effort, but bursting into a wild shrill laugh, pointed to it, exclaiming, "see there, see there, nice clothes!" Hot tears might not dissolve that iron bondage, imposed, to all appearance, most needlessly. As I left the room the poor creature said, "I want my gown! . . ."

Bolton. Late in December, 1842; thermometer 4° above zero; visited the almshouse; neat and comfortable establishment; two insane women, one in the house associated with the family, the other "*out of doors.*" . . . I asked to see the subject who was "out of doors;" and following the mistress of the house through the deep snow, shuddering and benumbed by the piercing cold, several hundred yards, we came in rear of the barn to a small building, which might have afforded a degree of comfortable shelter, but it did not. About two thirds of the interior was filled with wood and peat; the other third was divided into two parts, one about six feet square contained a cylinder stove, in which was no fire, the rusty pipe seeming to threaten, in its decay, either suffocation by smoke, which by and by we nearly realized, or conflagration of the building, together with destruction of its poor crazy inmate. My companion uttered an exclamation at finding no fire, and busied herself to light one, while I explored, as the deficient light permitted, the cage which occupied the undescribed portion of the building. "Oh, I'm so cold, so cold," was uttered in plaintive tones by a woman within the cage; "oh, so cold, so cold!" And well might she be cold; the stout, hardy, driver of the sleigh had declared 'twas too hard for a man to stand the wind and snow that day, yet here was a woman caged and imprisoned without fire or clothes, not naked indeed, for one thin cotton garment partly covered her, and part of a blanket was gathered about the shoulders; there she stood, shivering in that dreary place, the grey locks falling in disorder about the face gave a wild expression to the pallid features; untended and comfortless, she might call aloud, none could hear; she might die, and there be none to close the eye. But death would have been a blessing here. "Well, you shall have a fire, Axey; I've been so busy getting ready for the funeral!" One of the paupers lay dead. "Oh, I want some clothes," rejoined the lunatic; "I'm so cold." "Well, Axey, you shall have some as soon as the children come from school; I've had so much to do." "I want to go out, do let me out!" "Yes, as soon as I get time," answered the respondent. "Why do you keep her here?" I asked, "she appears harmless and quiet." "Well, I mean to take her up to the house pretty soon; the people that used to have care here, kept her sh⌐ ⌐ all the year; but it *is* cold here, and we take her to the house in hard weather; the only danger is her running away; I've been meaning to, this good while." The poor creature listened eagerly, "oh, I won't run away, do take me out!" "Well, I will in a few days." Now the smoke from the kindling fire became so dense that a new anxiety struck the captive; "oh, I shall smother, I'm afraid; don't fill that up, I'm afraid." Pretty soon I moved to go away; "stop, did you walk?" "No." "Did you ride?" "Yes." "Do take me with you, do, I'm so cold. Do you know my sisters? they live in this town; I want to see them so much; do let me go!" and shivering with eagerness to get out, as with the biting cold, she rapidly tried the bars of the cage. . . .

Of the dangers and mischiefs sometimes following the location of insane persons in our almhouses, I will record but one more example. In Worcester, has for several years resided a young woman, a lunatic pauper of decent life and respectable family. I have seen her as she usually appeared, listless and silent, almost or quite sunk into a state of dementia, sitting one amidst the family, "but not of them." A few weeks since, revisiting that almshouse, judge my horror and amazement to see her negligently bearing in her arms a young infant, of which I was told she was the unconscious parent! Who was the father, none could or would declare. . . .

It is not few but many, it is not a part but the whole, who bear unqualified testimony to this evil. A voice strong and deep comes up from every almshouse and prison in Massachusetts where the insane are or have been, protesting against such evils as have been illustrated in the preceding pages.

Respectfully submitted,
D. L. DIX.

85 Mt. Vernon St. Boston.
January, 1843.

from

Modern Persecution, or Insane Asylums Unveiled

ELIZABETH PARSONS WARE PACKARD

1873

The wife of a pastor and the mother of six children, Elizabeth Parsons Ware Packard was a formidable advocate for the rights of mentally ill women. At the age of twenty, she was hospitalized for mental illness and several years later was committed by her husband. Soon after Packard won her release in 1863, her husband left the state with their children. Undaunted, Packard adopted the cause of married women by lobbying state legislatures and writing books, copies of which she sold in advance to pay printing costs. Despite ongoing speculation about her psychological state, she eventually regained custody of her children. In this excerpt, Packard recounts alleged abuses she discovered during her asylum life.

Mrs. Cheneworth hung herself in her own room, after retiring from the dancing party, last night.

Her measure of grace was not sufficient to enable her to bear the accumulated burdens of her hard fate any longer. She was driven to desperation.

I cannot blame her for deliberately preferring death, to such a life as she has been experiencing in this asylum. She has literally been driven to it by abuse.

She was entered in my ward, where she remained for several weeks, when she was removed to the lowest ward, where she has been murdered by slow tortures.

If this institution is not responsible for the life of Mrs. Cheneworth, then I don't know what murder is.

She was evidently insane when she entered—she was not responsible, although her reason was not entirely dethroned. Her moral nature was keenly sensitive; her power of self-control was crushed by disease and medical maltreatment. She resisted until she evidently saw it was useless to expect justice, and was just crushed beneath this powerful despotism.

She was a lovely woman, fitted both by nature and education to be an ornament to society and her family. Gentle and confiding, with a high sense of honor and self-respect, she despised all degrading associations.

From her own representations, I inferred she had been the pet and pride of her parents—a kind of household goddess in her father's family. Under these benign influences her virtues were fostered, and she had the satisfaction of being loved and appreciated.

She had been quite a belle, and finally from her many admirers, she married one of her own, but not of her parents' choice. In him she seemed to have found everything her heart could desire. He both loved and appreciated her, as well he might.

She was small, delicately and gracefully formed, and peculiarly lady-like in her manners. She was a most accomplished dancer, having been trained in the school of the best French dancers in the country.

Her complexion white and clear, with regular features; dark but mild and tender eyes; hair long, black and glossy. In short she was a little, beautiful, fawn-like creature, when she came to this Institution.

She had been here a short time once before, after the birth of her first child; and from her account I inferred that her restoration to reason was not then attended with the grim spectre of horrors which must have inevitably accompanied this.

She had left a young babe, this time, which her physician advised her to wean, since she was now in a delicate condition. Thus her overtasked physical nature, abused as it was by bad medical treatment, added to the double burden she was called to endure, could not sustain the balance of her mental faculties.

Her nerves were unstrung, and lost their natural tone by the influence of opium, that most deadly foe of nature, which evidently caused her insanity.

The opium was expected to operate as a quietus to her then excited nervous system; but instead of this, it only increased her nervous irritability. The amount was then increased, and this course persisted in, until her system became drunk, as it were, by its influence. The effect produced was like that of excessive drinking, when it causes delirium tremens. Thus she became a victim to that absurd practice of the medical profession, which depends upon poisons instead of nature to cure disease.

It is not natural to cure disease by creating disease. To poison nature, is not the natural way to eradicate poison from the system. To load nature with additional burdens, is not the way to lighten its previous burdens.

But common sense dictates that the natural way to aid nature in throwing off her diseases, is to strengthen the powers of healing, and thereby directly assist her in curing disease.

Nature's energies are strengthened, renewed and nourished by rest, quiet, sleep, food, air, cleanliness, freedom, exercise, etc.; and medical skill consists in adapting these agencies to their peculiar functions, so that the special want of nature may be met by its natural supply.

What Mrs. Cheneworth wanted, was the nourishment of her exhausted physical nature, by rest, food, air, and exercise.

She did not need to have the powers of her system thrown into confusion by taxing them with poisons, which nature must either counteract and resist, or be overcome by them, and sink into death. Nature was importuning for help to bear her burdens, being already overtasked.

But instead of listening to these demands, her blinded friends allowed her to be thus medically abused. After having suffered her to receive this treatment, which brought into a still worse condition—an insane state—when more than ever she need help and the most tender, watchful care; then to be cast off in helplessness upon strangers, who knew nothing of her character, her habits, her propensities, her cravings, her disposition, or her constitution; how could they reasonably expect her thus to receive the care necessary to her recovery?

They probably did expect it, and on this false basis placed her here for appropriate medical treatment. . . .

Why cannot their friends bestow upon them this "medical treatment" at home, without the expense of sending them to the Lunatic Asylum? . . .

Mrs. Cheneworth is only one among many, many others which her case represents. During the few weeks she was in my ward, after she first came, she was kindly treated. Perhaps her own parents could not have done better by her, than did Miss Tomlin and Miss McKelva, so far as their limited powers extended.

They could not grant her that liberty and freedom she so panted for, nor could they gratify her longings to see her own offspring, and bestow upon them the love of her maternal heart; nor could they bring to her the sympathy of her fond mother, for which she so ardently longed; neither could they summon to her side her husband— her chosen protector—who had sworn before God never to forsake her in sickness or in health, although it was her most earnest wish that he might come and see her condition for himself.

No, neither of these influences could these attendants summon for her relief or benefit; but so far as the ward duties extended, they did as well by her as they could.

I never saw either of them get the least angry or impatient towards her, although she tried them exceedingly by her antics. They seemed to feel that instead of getting angry at an insane person, they were placed here to "Bear the infirmities of the weak, and not to please themselves."

I feel that they have nothing to dread in the revelations of Mrs. Cheneworth's Asylum discipline. Of each of them I trust the Judge will say, "she hath done what she could" for her suffering sister.

These attendants are highly cultivated, well developed women, who could enter into Mrs. Cheneworth's feelings, and sympathize with her in her trials. They not only knew   v to treat her nature, but their principles controlled their feelings,   hat her trials might not be increased by any injudicious act on their part. Neither did they seem to despise her for being so sorely afflicted, but pitied and longed to help her.

Alas! for poor Mrs. Cheneworth! her days for reasonable treatment expired when she was removed to the lowest ward, and consigned to the care of Elizabeth Bonner.

This attendant was a perfect contrast to her former attendants in character, disposition, and habits. She was a large, coarse, stout Irish woman, stronger than most men; of quick temper, very easily thrown off its balance, when, for the time being, she would be a perfect demon, lost to all traces of humanity. Her manners were very coarse and masculine, a loud and boisterous talker, and a great liar, with no education, and could neither read nor write.

To this vile, ignorant woman was Mrs. Cheneworth entrusted, to be treated just as her own feelings dictated.

Miss Bonner's first object was to "subdue her," that is, to break down her aspiring feelings, and bring her into a state of cringing submission to her dictation.

Here was a contest between her naturally refined instincts, and Miss Bonner's unrefined and coarse nature. Any manifestation of the lady-like nature of Mrs. Cheneworth, was met by its opposite in Miss Bonner's servant-like nature and position, and she must lord it over this gentle lady.

The position of the latter, as a boarder, must, at her beck, be exchanged, by her being made to feel that she was nothing but a slave and menial. If she ventured to remonstrate against this wanton usurpation of authority over her, she could only expect to receive physical abuse, such as she was poorly able to bear.

And Oh! the black tale of wrongs and cruel tortures this tender woman experienced at the hand of this giant-like tyrant, no tongue or pen can ever describe!

She was choked, pounded, kicked, and plunged under water, until well nigh strangled to death.

Mrs. Coe assured me this was only a specimen of the kind of treatment all were liable to receive at her hands, since she claimed that this was the way to cure them! and this she insisted   n, was what she was put here to do.

Being strong, she was peculiarly adapted to her place, since no woman or man could grapple with her successfully.

This is the attendant who so often made it her boast that Dr. McFarland let her do with the patients just as she chose—that her judgment, her feelings, and her temper could be trusted in all cases!

Oh! what is there of injury and physical abuse that this institution will not have to answer for, which has not been inflicted by brutal attendants—while Dr. McFarland has sustained them by knowingly approving of these things?

I do not believe the trustees would knowingly sustain these brutalities. But Dr. McFarland's statements are regarded by them as infallibly correct, and as he represents the treatment here bestowed upon the patients, they doubtless feel confident that they are humanely treated. But did they know what I know, I believe they would disapprove of it, and not like Dr. McFarland, try to cover it up, lest the interests of the institution be jeopardized by the investigation.

The facts I have already placed before them in a written form, would of themselves arouse their interest and summon their immediate investigation, did they not so implicitly rely upon the Doctor's contradiction as proof of their fallacy!

In this way they are believing lies, and under this delusion they are not only winking at iniquities, but publicly sustaining them. It is in their power to ascertain the truth, did they feel determined to know for themselves. But this investigation would be attended with more trouble and inconvenience than it is to let it go on, and thereby these slothful servants of the public are justly held responsible for the sins of this house.

Poor Mrs. Cheneworth could not await this retribution, but was driven to seek the only defence within her reach, death! yes, death—the most dreadful of all evils—was chosen rather than such a life as she was doomed to endure under the rule of this Inquisition.

I cannot, no, I cannot blame her for killing herself. I do not think God will blame her. She was like one who deliberately rushed into the flames, to escape the barbed arrows of an invincible foe. She only chose the quicker, rather than the lingerin ;onizing death, to which she seemed inevitably doomed, at the han of Elizabeth Bonner.

The last time I saw Mrs. Cheneworth was at the dance, after which she hung herself, being found suspended from the upper part of her window by the facing of her dress.

I never saw a person so changed. I did not know her when Miss Bonner introduced me to her that evening. Such a haggard look! such despair and wretchedness as her countenance reflected, I have never witnessed. My feelings were touched.

I asked her to go with me, and putting my arm around her waist, she walked with me across the ward to the window looking South. Here we conversed confidentially, freely. She said:

"Oh! Mrs. Packard, I have suffered everything but death since we were parted!"

"But how has your face become so disfigured by sores, and what causes your eyes to be so inflamed?"

"I fainted, and fell down stairs, and they poured camphor so profusely over my face, and into my eyes and ears, that I have, in consequence, been blind and deaf for some time."

I do not know whether her chin, which was red and raw, was thus caused or not. She said the fall had caused her to miscarry, and thus, thought I, you have had to bear this burden in addition to the load of sorrows already heaped upon your tender, weak person. Said I:

"Have you any hope of getting out of this place—of ever being taken to your friends?"

"No! none at all! Hopeless, endless torment is all that is before me! Oh, if I could only get out of this place, I would walk to my father's house. It is only fourteen miles south, here," pointing out of the window, "but Oh, these iron bars! I cannot escape through them."

How I did pity her! But I could only say, as I do to others:

"Do try to be patient as you can; for I do hope this house will not long stand, and that in its destruction, we may be delivered out of this place of torment."

I had no other tangible hope to offer her drooping heart already deadly sick from hope too long deferred. She said:

"I wish I could get into the ward with you; I will ask Dr. McFarland, to-morrow, to remove me there."

"Alas!" thought I, "no request of yours will b   :eded, as a source of relief to you; for it is not to relieve, but to torment you, that you are kept here. Could I but inform your parents of their dear daughter's sad fate, surely they would come to your rescue."

Then I thought of the letter I had sent to Mrs. Timmons' friends in her behalf, and how, like deaf adders, they would not hear, or would not believe my statements, unless endorsed by Dr. McFarland. I turned away, sick at heart, at sight of woes I could not mitigate or remove.

Oh, when will the prisoner's bonds be loosed and the lawful captive be delivered?

Notwithstanding, I think I offered to intercede for her, while, at the same time, I knew it would be utterly fruitless, as I have so often tried reason, argument and entreaty, only to find it useless.

"Yes, sister, I cannot but congratulate you on what I believe to be your happy exchange; for I do not think you can find, in all the universe, a worse place of torment than you found here. May'st thou find that rest in death that was denied thee on earth."

from

Ten Days in a Mad-House, or Nellie Bly's Experiences on Blackwell's Island

ELIZABETH COCHRANE

1887

While on assignment for the World *in New York City, journalist Elizabeth Cochrane feigned insanity in order to gain access to a local asylum, Blackwell's Island. Her account, written under the pen name "Nellie Bly," is one of the earliest newspaper investigations of the treatment mental patients received behind the walls of insane asylums. In this excerpt, Cochrane, posing as "Nellie Brown," reports on her brief stay at Bellevue Hospital, where she was pronounced "positively demented" before being sent to Blackwell's Island. After the publication of her exposé, New York City appropriated an additional $1 million per year to improve services for the mentally ill. Three years later, Cochrane wrote about her now-famous voyage in* Nellie Bly's Book: Around the World in Seventy-two Days.

... The ambulance stopped with a sudden jerk and the doctor jumped out. "How many have you?" I heard some one inquire. "Only one, for the pavilion," was the reply. A rough-looking   came forward, and catching hold of me attempted to drag me out   f I had the strength of an elephant and would resist. The doctor, seeing my look of disgust, ordered him to leave me alone, saying that he would take charge of me himself. He then lifted me carefully out and I walked with the grace of a queen past the crowd that had gathered curious to see the new unfortunate. Together with the doctor I entered a small dark office, where there were several men. The one behind the desk opened a book and began on the long string of questions which had been asked me so often.

I refused to answer, and the doctor told him it was not necessary to trouble me further, as he had all the papers made out, and I was too insane to be able to tell anything that would be of consequence. I felt relieved that it was so easy here, as, though still undaunted, I had begun to feel faint for want of food. The order was then given to take me to the insane pavilion, and a muscular man came forward and caught me so tightly by the arm that a pain ran clear through me. It made me angry, and for a moment I forgot my *role* as I turned to him and said:

"How dare you touch me?" At this he loosened his hold somewhat, and I shook him off with more strength than I thought I possessed.

"I will go with no one but this man," I said, pointing to the ambulance-surgeon. "The judge said that he was to take care of me, and I will go with no one else."

At this the surgeon said that he would take me, and so we went arm in arm, following the man who had at first been so rough with me. We passed through the well-cared-for grounds and finally reached the insane ward. A white-capped nurse was there to receive me.

"This young girl is to wait here for the boat," said the surgeon, and then he started to leave me. I begged him not to go, or to take me with him, but he said he wanted to get his dinner first, and that I should wait there for him. When I insisted on accompanying him he claimed that he had to assist at an amputation, and it would not look well for me to be present. It was evident that he believed he was dealing with an insane person. Just then the most horrible insane cries came from a yard in the rear. With all my bravery I felt a chill at the prospect of being shut up with a fellow-creature who was really insane. The doctor evidently noticed my nervousness, for he said the attendant:

"What a noise the carpenters make."

Turning to me he offered me explanation to the effect that new buildings were being erected, and that the noise came from some of the workmen engaged upon it. I told him I did not want to stay there without him, and to pacify me he promised soon to return. He left me and I found myself at last an occupant of an insane asylum.

I stood at the door and contemplated the scene before me. The long, uncarpeted hall was scrubbed to that peculiar whiteness seen only in public institutions. In the rear of the hall were large iron doors fastened by a padlock. Several stiff-looking benches and a number of willow chairs were the only articles of furniture. On either side of the hall were doors leading into what I supposed and what proved to be bedrooms. Near the entrance door, on the right-hand side, was a small sitting-room for the nurses, and opposite it was a room where dinner was dished out. A nurse in a black dress, white cap and apron and armed with a bunch of keys had charge of the hall. I soon learned her name, Miss Ball.

An old Irish woman was maid-of-all-work. I heard her called Mary, and I am glad to know that there is such a good-hearted woman in that place. I experienced only kindness and the utmost consideration from her. There were only three patients, as they are called. I made the fourth. I thought I might as well begin work at once, for I still expected that the very first doctor might declare me sane and send me out again into the wide, wide world. So I went down to the rear of the room and introduced myself to one of the women, and asked her all about herself. Her name, she said, was Miss Anne Neville, and she had been sick from overwork. She had been working as a chambermaid, and when her health gave way she was sent to some Sisters' Home to be treated. Her nephew, who was a waiter, was out of work, and, being unable to pay her expenses at the Home, had had her transferred to Bellevue.

"Is there anything wrong with you mentally as well?" I asked her.

"No," she said. "The doctors have been asking me many curious questions and confusing me as much as possible, but I have nothing wrong with my brain."

"Do you know that only insane people are sent to this pavilion?" I asked.

"Yes, I know; but I am unable to do anything. The doctors refuse to listen to me, and it is useless to say anything to the nurses."

Satisfied from various reasons that Miss Neville was as sane as I was myself, I transferred my attentions to one of the other patients. I found her in need of medical aid and quite silly mentally, although I have seen many women in the lower walks of life, whose sanity was never questioned, who were not any brighter.

The third patient, Mrs. Fox, would not say much. She was very quiet, and after telling me that her case was hopeless refused to talk. I began now to feel surer of my position, and I determined that no doctor should convince me that I was sane so long as I had the hope of accomplishing my mission. A small, fair-complexioned nurse arrived, and, after putting on her cap, told Miss Ball to go to dinner. The new nurse, Miss Scott by name, came to me and said, rudely:

"Take off your hat."

"I shall not take off my hat," I answered. "I am waiting for the boat, and I shall not remove it."

"Well, you are not going on any boat. You might as well know it now as later. You are in an asylum for the insane."

Although fully aware of that fact, her unvarnished words gave me a shock. "I did not want to come here: I am not sick or insane, and I will not stay," I said.

"It will be a long time before you get out if you don't do as you are told," answered Miss Scott. "You might as well take off your hat, or I shall use force, and if I am not able to do it, I have but to touch a bell and I shall get assistance. Will you take it off?"

"No, I will not. I am cold, and I want my hat on and you can't make me take it off."

"I shall give you a few more minutes, and if you don't take it off then I shall use force, and I warn you it will not be very gentle."

"If you take my hat off I shall take your cap off; so now."

Miss Scott was called to the door then, and as I feared that an exhibition of temper might show too much sanity I took off my hat and gloves and was sitting quietly looking into space when she returned. I was hungry, and was quite pleased to see Mary make preparations for dinner. The preparations were simple. She merely pulled a straight bench up along the side of a bare table   ordered the patients to gather 'round the feast; then she brought o   small tin plate on which was a piece of boiled meat and a potato. It could not have been colder had it been cooked the week before, and it had no chance to make acquaintance with salt or pepper. I would not go up to the table, so Mary came to where I sat in a corner, and, while handing out the tin plate, asked:

"Have ye any pennies about ye, dearie?"

"What?" I said, in my surprise.

"Have ye any pennies, dearie, that ye could give me. They'll take them all from ye any way, dearie, so I might as well have them."

I understood it fully now, but I had no intention of feeing Mary so early in the game, fearing it would have an influence on her treatment of me, so I said I had lost my purse, which was quite true. But though I did not give Mary any money, she was none the less kind to me. When I objected to the tin plate in which she had brought my food she fetched a china one for me, and when I found it impossible to eat the food she presented she gave me a glass of milk and a soda cracker.

All the windows in the hall were open and the cold air began to tell on my Southern blood. It grew so cold indeed as to be almost unbearable, and I complained of it to Miss Scott and Miss Ball. But they answered curtly that as I was in a charity place I could not expect much else. All the other women were suffering from the cold, and the nurses themselves had to wear heavy garments to keep themselves warm. I asked if I could go to bed. They said "No!" At last Miss Scott got an old gray shawl, and shaking some of the moths out of it, told me to put it on.

"It's rather a bad-looking shawl," I said.

"Well, some people would get along better if they were not so proud," said Miss Scott. "People on charity should not expect anything and should not complain."

So I put the moth-eaten shawl, with all its musty smell, around me, and sat down on a wicker chair, wondering what would come next, whether I should freeze to death or survive. My nose was very cold, so I covered up my head and was in a half doze, when the shawl was suddenly jerked from my face and a strange man and Miss Scott stood before me. The man proved to be a doctor, and his first greetings were:

"I've seen that face before."

"Then you know me?" I asked, with a great   w of eagerness that I did not feel.

"I think I do. Where did you come from?"

"From home."

"Where is home?"

"Don't you know? Cuba."

He then sat down beside me, felt my pulse, and examined my tongue, and at last said:

"Tell Miss Scott all about yourself."

"No, I will not. I will not talk with women."

"What do you do in New York?"

"Nothing."

"Can you work?"

"No, senor."

"Tell me, are you a woman of the town?"

"I do not understand you," I replied, heartily disgusted with him.

"I mean have you allowed the men to provide for you and keep you?"

I felt like slapping him in the face, but I had to maintain my composure, so I simply said:

"I do not know what you are talking about. I always lived at home."

After many more questions, fully as useless and senseless, he left me and began to talk with the nurse. "Positively demented," he said. "I consider it a hopeless case. She needs to be put where some one will take care of her."

And so I passed my second medical expert.

After this, I began to have a smaller regard for the ability of doctors than I ever had before, and a greater one for myself. I felt sure now that no doctor could tell whether people were insane or not, so long as the case was not violent.

Later in the afternoon a boy and a woman came. The woman sat down on a bench, while the boy went in and talked with Miss Scott. In a short time he came out, and, just nodding good-bye to the woman, who was his mother, went away. She did not look insane, but as she was German I could not learn her story. Her name, however, was Mrs. Louise Schanz. She seemed quite lost, but ̇ en the nurses put her at some sewing she did her work well and q̇ ̇ly. At three in the afternoon all the patients were given a gruel broth, and at five a cup of tea and a piece of bread. I was favored; for when they saw that it was impossible for me to eat the bread or drink the stuff honored by the name of tea, they gave me a cup of milk and a cracker, the same as I had had at noon.

Just as the gas was being lighted another patient was added. She was a young girl, twenty-five years old. She told me that she had just gotten up from a sick bed. Her appearance confirmed her story. She looked like one who had had a severe attack of fever. "I am now suffering from nervous debility," she said, "and my friends have sent me here to be treated for it." I did not tell her where she was, and she seemed quite satisfied. At 6.15 Miss Ball said that she wanted to go away, and so we would all have to go to bed. Then each of us—we now numbered six—were assigned a room and told to undress. I did so, and was given a short, cotton-flannel gown to wear during the night. Then she took every particle of the clothing I had worn during the day, and, making it up in a bundle, labeled it "Brown," and took it away. The iron-barred window was locked, and Miss Ball, after giving me an extra blanket, which, she said, was a favor rarely granted, went out and left me alone. The bed was not a comfortable one. It was so hard, indeed, that I could not make a dent in it; and the pillow was stuffed with straw. Under the sheet was an oilcloth spread. As the night grew colder I tried to warm that oilcloth. I kept on trying, but when morning dawned and it was still as cold as when I went to bed, and had reduced me, too, to the temperature of an iceberg, I gave it up as an impossible task.

I had hoped to get some rest on this my first night in an insane asylum. But I was doomed to disappointment. When the night nurses came in they were curious to see me and to find out what I was like. . . . I listened quite anxiously to the talk about me, and was relieved to learn that I was considered hopelessly insane. That was encouraging. I heard new arrivals, and I learned that a doctor was there and intended to see me. For what purpose I knew not, and I imagined all sorts of horrible things, such as examinations and the rest of it, and when they got to my room I was shaking with more than ˉ

"Nellie Brown, here is the doctor; he wish   o speak with you," said the nurse. If that's all he wanted I thought I could endure it. I removed the blanket which I had put over my head in my sudden fright and looked up. The sight was reassuring.

He was a handsome young man. He had the air and address of a gentleman. Some people have since censured this action; but I feel sure, even if it was a little indiscreet, that the young doctor only meant kindness to me. He came forward, seated himself on the side of my bed, and put his arm soothingly around my shoulders. It was a terrible task to play insane before this young man, and only a girl can sympathize with me in my position.

"How do you feel to-night, Nellie?" he asked, easily.

"Oh, I feel all right."

"But you are sick, you know," he said.

"Oh, am I?" I replied, and I turned my head on the pillow and smiled.

"When did you leave Cuba, Nellie?"

"Oh, you know my home?" I asked.

"Yes, very well. Don't you remember me? I remember you."

"Do you?" and I mentally said I should not forget him. He was accompanied by a friend who never ventured a remark, but stood staring at me as I lay in bed. After a great many questions, to which I answered truthfully, he left me. Then came other troubles. All night long the nurses read one to the other aloud, and I know that the other patients, as well as myself, were unable to sleep. Every half-hour or hour they would walk heavily down the halls, their boot-heels resounding like the march of a private of dragoons, and take a look at every patient. Of course this helped to keep us awake. Then, as it came toward morning, they began to beat eggs for breakfast, and the sound made me realize how horribly hungry I was. Occasional yells and cries came from the male department, and that did not aid in making the night pass more cheerfully. Then the ambulance-gong, as it brought in more unfortunates, sounded as a knell to life and liberty.

"THE YELLOW WALLPAPER"

CHARLOTTE PERKINS STETSON GILMAN

1892

After seeking treatment from a well-known Philadelphia "nerve spe-
cialist," Charlotte Perkins Stetson wrote her autobiographical short
story, "The Yellow Wallpaper." Magazine editors initially rejected her
work, with rebuffs such as Horace Scudder's of the Atlantic
Monthly: *"I could not forgive myself if I made others as miserable as*
I have made myself!" Eventually published by the New England
Magazine *in 1892, "The Yellow Wallpaper" is now considered a*
classic portrayal of the mental anguish suffered by oppressed
nineteenth-century women. Gilman, a poet, editor, and writer of fiction
and nonfiction, also lectured widely on women's rights. After divorcing
her first husband, she married her cousin George H. Gilman in 1900.
Ailing from breast cancer, she committed suicide in 1935.

It is very seldom that mere ordinary people like John and myself secure ancestral halls for the summer.

A colonial mansion, a hereditary estate, I would say a haunted
house, and reach the height of romantic felicity—but that would be
asking too much of fate!

Still I will proudly declare that there is something queer about it.

Else, why should it be let so cheaply? And why have stood so long
untenanted?

John laughs at me, of course, but one expects that in marriage.

John is practical in the extreme. He has no patience with faith, an
intense horror of superstition, and he scoffs openly at any talk of
things not to be felt and seen and put down in figures.

John is a physician, and *perhaps*—(I would not say it to a living soul, of course, but this is dead paper and a great relief to my mind)—*perhaps* that is one reason I do not get well faster.

You see he does not believe I am sick!

And what can one do?

If a physician of high standing, and one's own husband, assures friends and relatives that there is really nothing the matter with one but temporary nervous depression—a slight hysterical tendency—what is one to do?

My brother is also a physician, and also of high standing, and he says the same thing.

So I take phosphates or phospites—whichever it is, and tonics, and journeys, and air, and exercise, and am absolutely forbidden to "work" until I am well again.

Personally, I disagree with their ideas.

Personally, I believe that congenial work, with excitement and change, would do me good.

But what is one to do?

I did write for a while in spite of them; but it *does* exhaust me a good deal—having to be so sly about it, or else meet with heavy opposition.

I sometimes fancy that in my condition if I had less opposition and more society and stimulus—but John says the very worst thing I can do is to think about my condition, and I confess it always makes me feel bad.

So I will let it alone and talk about the house.

The most beautiful place! It is quite alone, standing well back from the road, quite three miles from the village. It makes me think of English places that you read about, for there are hedges and walls and gates that lock, and lots of separate little houses f he gardeners and people.

There is a *delicious* garden! I never saw ch a garden—large and shady, full of box-bordered paths, and lined with long grape-covered arbors with seats under them.

There were greenhouses, too, but they are all broken now.

There was some legal trouble, I believe, something about the heirs and coheirs; anyhow, the place has been empty for years.

That spoils my ghostliness, I am afraid, but I don't care—there is something strange about the house—I can feel it.

I even said so to John one moonlight evening, but he said what I felt was a *draught,* and shut the window.

I get unreasonably angry with John sometimes. I'm sure I never used to be so sensitive. I think it is due to this nervous condition.

But John says if I feel so, I shall neglect proper self-control; so I take pains to control myself—before him, at least, and that makes me very tired.

I don't like our room a bit. I wanted one downstairs that opened on the piazza and had roses all over the window, and such pretty old-fashioned chintz hangings! but John would not hear of it.

He said there was only one window and not room for two beds, and no near room for him if he took another.

He is very careful and loving, and hardly lets me stir without special direction.

I have a schedule prescription for each hour in the day; he takes all care from me, and so I feel basely ungrateful not to value it more.

He said we came here solely on my account, that I was to have perfect rest and all the air I could get. "Your exercise depends on your strength, my dear," said he, "and your food somewhat on your appetite; but air you can absorb all the time." So we took the nursery at the top of the house.

It is a big, airy room, the whole floor nearly, with windows that look all ways, and air and sunshine galore. It was nursery first and then playroom and gymnasium, I should judge; for the windows are barred for little children, and there are rings and things in the walls.

The paint and paper look as if a boys' school had used it. It is stripped off—the paper—in great patches all   ınd the head of my bed, about as far as I can reach, and in a great ı ːe on the other side of the room low down. I never saw a worse paper in my life.

One of those sprawling flamboyant patterns committing every artistic sin.

It is dull enough to confuse the eye in following, pronounced enough to constantly irritate and provoke study, and when you follow the lame uncertain curves for a little distance they suddenly commit suicide—plunge off at outrageous angles, destroy themselves in unheard of contradictions.

The color is repellent, almost revolting; a smouldering unclean yellow, strangely faded by the slow-turning sunlight.

It is a dull yet lurid orange in some places, a sickly sulphur tint in others.

No wonder the children hated it! I should hate it myself if I had to live in this room long.

There comes John, and I must put this away,—he hates to have me write a word.

———

We have been here two weeks, and I haven't felt like writing before, since that first day.

I am sitting by the window now, up in this atrocious nursery, and there is nothing to hinder my writing as much as I please, save lack of strength.

John is away all day, and even some nights when his cases are serious.

I am glad my case is not serious!

But these nervous troubles are dreadfully depressing.

John does not know how much I really suffer. He knows there is no *reason* to suffer, and that satisfies him.

Of course it is only nervousness. It does weigh on me so not to do my duty in any way!

I meant to be such a help to John, such a real rest and comfort, and here I am a comparative burden already!

Nobody would believe what an effort it is to do what little I am able,—to dress and entertain, and order things.

It is fortunate Mary is so good with the baby. Such a dear baby!

And yet I *cannot* be with him, it makes me so nervous.

I suppose John never was nervous in his life. He laughs at me so about this wall-paper!

At first he meant to repaper the room, but afterwards he said that I was letting it get the better of me, and that nothing was worse for a nervous patient than to give way to such fancies.

He said that after the wall-paper was changed it would be the heavy bedstead, and then the barred windows, and then that gate at the head of the stairs, and so on.

"You know the place is doing you good," he said, "and really, dear, I don't care to renovate the house just for a three months' rental."

"Then do let us go downstairs," I said, "there are such pretty rooms there."

Then he took me in his arms and called me a blessed little goose, and said he would go down to the cellar, if I wished, and have it white-washed into the bargain.

But he is right enough about the beds and windows and things.

It is an airy and comfortable room as any one need wish, and, of course, I would not be so silly as to make him uncomfortable just for a whim.

I'm really getting quite fond of the big room, all but that horrid paper.

Out of one window I can see the garden, those mysterious deepshaded arbors, the riotous old-fashioned flowers, and bushes and gnarly trees.

Out of another I get a lovely view of the bay and a little private wharf belonging to the estate. There is a beautiful shaded lane that runs down there from the house. I always fancy I see people walking in these numerous paths and arbors, but John has cautioned me not to give way to fancy in the least. He says that with my imaginative power and habit of story-making, a nervous weakness like mine is sure to lead to all manner of excited fancies, and that I ought to use my will and good sense to check the tendency. So I try.

I think sometimes that if I were only well enough to write a little it would relieve the press of ideas and rest me.

But I find I get pretty tired when I try.

It is so discouraging not to have any advi   nd companionship about my work. When I get really well, John says we will ask Cousin Henry and Julia down for a long visit; but he says he would as soon put fireworks in my pillow-case as to let me have those stimulating people about now.

I wish I could get well faster.

But I must not think about that. This paper looks to me as if it *knew* what a vicious influence it had!

There is a recurrent spot where the pattern lolls like a broken neck and two bulbous eyes stare at you upside down.

I get positively angry with the impertinence of it and the everlastingness. Up and down and sideways they crawl, and those absurd, unblinking eyes are everywhere. There is one place where two breadths didn't match, and the eyes go all up and down the line, one a little higher than the other.

I never saw so much expression in an inanimate thing before, and we all know how much expression they have! I used to lie awake as a child and get more entertainment and terror out of blank walls and plain furniture than most children could find in a toy-store.

I remember what a kindly wink the knobs of our big, old bureau used to have, and there was one chair that always seemed like a strong friend.

I used to feel that if any of the other things looked too fierce I could always hop into that chair and be safe.

The furniture in this room is no worse than inharmonious, however, for we had to bring it all from downstairs. I suppose when this was used as a playroom they had to take the nursery things out, and no wonder! I never saw such ravages as the children have made here.

The wall-paper, as I said before, is torn off in spots, and it sticketh closer than a brother—they must have had perseverance as well as hatred.

Then the floor is scratched and gouged and splintered, the plaster itself is dug out here and there, and this great heavy bed which is all we found in the room, looks as if it had been through the wars.

But I don't mind it a bit—only the paper.

There comes John's sister. Such a dear   as she is, and so careful of me! I must not let her find me writing.

She is a perfect and enthusiastic housekeeper, and hopes for no better profession. I verily believe she thinks it is the writing which made me sick!

But I can write when she is out, and see her a long way off from these windows.

There is one that commands the road, a lovely shaded winding road, and one that just looks off over the country. A lovely country, too, full of great elms and velvet meadows.

This wall-paper has a kind of sub-pattern in a different shade, a particularly irritating one, for you can only see it in certain lights, and not clearly then.

But in the places where it isn't faded and where the sun is just so— I can see a strange, provoking, formless sort of figure, that seems to skulk about behind that silly and conspicuous front design.

There's sister on the stairs!

———

Well, the Fourth of July is over! The people are all gone and I am tired out. John thought it might do me good to see a little company, so we just had mother and Nellie and the children down for a week.

Of course I didn't do a thing. Jennie sees to everything now.

But it tired me all the same.

John says if I don't pick up faster he shall send me to Weir Mitchell in the fall.

But I don't want to go there at all. I had a friend who was in his hands once, and she says he is just like John and my brother, only more so!

Besides, it is such an undertaking to go so far.

I don't feel as if it was worth while to turn my hand over for any-thing, and I'm getting dreadfully fretful and querulous.

I cry at nothing, and cry most of the time.

Of course I don't when John is here, or anybody else, but when I am alone.

And I am alone a good deal just now. John is kept in town very often by serious cases, and Jennie is good and lets me alone when I want her to.

So I walk a little in the garden or down that lovely lane, sit on the porch under the roses, and lie down up here a good deal.

I'm getting really fond of the room in spite of the wall-paper. Per-haps *because* of the wall-paper.

It dwells in my mind so!

I lie here on this great immovable bed—it is nailed down, I

believe—and follow that pattern about by the hour. It is as good as gymnastics, I assure you. I start, we'll say, at the bottom, down in the corner over there where it has not been touched, and I determine for the thousandth time that I *will* follow that pointless pattern to some sort of a conclusion.

I know a little of the principle of design, and I know this thing was not arranged on any laws of radiation, or alternation, or repetition, or symmetry, or anything else that I ever heard of.

It is repeated, of course, by the breadths, but not otherwise.

Looked at in one way each breadth stands alone, the bloated curves and flourishes—a kind of "debased Romanesque" with *delirium tremens*—go waddling up and down in isolated columns of fatuity.

But, on the other hand, they connect diagonally, and the sprawling outlines run off in great slanting waves of optic horror, like a lot of wallowing seaweeds in full chase.

The whole thing goes horizontally, too, at least it seems so, and I exhaust myself in trying to distinguish the order of its going in that direction.

They have used a horizontal breadth for a frieze, and that adds wonderfully to the confusion.

There is one end of the room where it is almost intact, and there, when the crosslights fade and the low sun shines directly upon it, I can almost fancy radiation after all,—the interminable grotesques seem to form around a common centre and rush off in headlong plunges of equal distraction.

It makes me tired to follow it. I will take a nap I guess.

I don't know why I should write this.

I don't want to.

I don't feel able.

And I know John would think it absur ut I *must* say what I feel and think in some way—it is such a relief

But the effort is getting to be greater than the relief.

Half the time now I am awfully lazy, and lie down ever so much.

John says I mustn't lose my strength, and has me take cod liver oil and lots of tonics and things, to say nothing of ale and wine and rare meat.

Dear John! He loves me very dearly, and hates to have me sick. I tried to have a real earnest reasonable talk with him the other day, and tell him how I wish he would let me go and make a visit to Cousin Henry and Julia.

But he said I wasn't able to go, nor able to stand it after I got there; and I did not make out a very good case for myself, for I was crying before I had finished.

It is getting to be a great effort for me to think straight. Just this nervous weakness I suppose.

And dear John gathered me up in his arms, and just carried me upstairs and laid me on the bed, and sat by me and read to me till it tired my head.

He said I was his darling and his comfort and all he had, and that I must take care of myself for his sake, and keep well.

He says no one but myself can help me out of it, that I must use my will and self-control and not let any silly fancies run away with me.

There's one comfort, the baby is well and happy, and does not have to occupy this nursery with the horrid wall-paper.

If we had not used it, that blessed child would have! What a fortunate escape! Why, I wouldn't have a child of mine, an impressionable little thing, live in such a room for worlds.

I never thought of it before, but it is lucky that John kept me here after all, I can stand it so much easier than a baby, you see.

Of course I never mention it to them any more—I am too wise,—but I keep watch of it all the same.

There are things in that paper that nobody knows but me, or ever will.

Behind that outside pattern the dim shapes get clearer every day.

It is always the same shape, only very nume   s.

And it is like a woman stooping down and   eping about behind that pattern. I don't like it a bit. I wonder—I begin to think—I wish John would take me away from here!

It is so hard to talk with John about my case, because he is so wise, and because he loves me so.

But I tried it last night.

It was moonlight. The moon shines in all around just as the sun does.

I hate to see it sometimes, it creeps so slowly, and always comes in by one window or another.

John was asleep and I hated to waken him, so I kept still and watched the moonlight on that undulating wall-paper till I felt creepy.

The faint figure behind seemed to shake the pattern, just as if she wanted to get out.

I got up softly and went to feel and see if the paper *did* move, and when I came back John was awake.

"What is it, little girl?" he said. "Don't go walking about like that— you'll get cold."

I thought it was a good time to talk, so I told him that I really was not gaining here, and that I wished he would take me away.

"Why, darling!" said he, "our lease will be up in three weeks, and I can't see how to leave before.

"The repairs are not done at home, and I cannot possibly leave town just now. Of course if you were in any danger, I could and would, but you really are better, dear, whether you can see it or not. I am a doctor, dear, and I know. You are gaining flesh and color, your appetite is better, I feel really much easier about you."

"I don't weigh a bit more," said I, "nor as much; and my appetite may be better in the evening when you are here, but it is worse in the morning when you are away!"

"Bless her little heart!" said he with a big hug, "she shall be as sick as she pleases! But now let's improve the shining hours by going to sleep, and talk about it in the morning!"

"And you won't go away?" I asked gloomily.

"Why, how can I, dear? It is only three weeks more and then we will take a nice little trip of a few days while Jennie is getting the house ready. Really dear you are better!"

"Better in body perhaps—" I began, and stopped short, for he sat up straight and looked at me with such a stern, reproachful look that I could not say another word.

"My darling," said he, "I beg of you, for my sake and for our child's sake, as well as for your own, that you will never for one instant let that idea enter your mind! There is nothing so dangerous, so fascinating, to a temperament like yours. It is a false and foolish fancy. Can you not trust me as a physician when I tell you so?"

So of course I said no more on that score, and we went to sleep before long. He thought I was asleep first, but I wasn't, and lay there for hours trying to decide whether that front pattern and the back pattern really did move together or separately.

———

On a pattern like this, by daylight, there is a lack of sequence, a defiance of law, that is a constant irritant to a normal mind.

The color is hideous enough, and unreliable enough, and infuriating enough, but the pattern is torturing.

You think you have mastered it, but just as you get well underway in following, it turns a back-somersault and there you are. It slaps you in the face, knocks you down, and tramples upon you. It is like a bad dream.

The outside pattern is a florid arabesque, reminding one of a fungus. If you can imagine a toadstool in joints, an interminable string of toadstools, budding and sprouting in endless convolutions—why, that is something like it.

That is, sometimes!

There is one marked peculiarity about this paper, a thing nobody seems to notice but myself, and that is that it changes as the light changes.

When the sun shoots in through the east window—I always watch for that first long, straight ray—it changes so quickly that I never can quite believe it.

That is why I watch it always.

By moonlight—the moon shines in all t when there is a moon—I wouldn't know it was the same pape

At night in any kind of light, in twilight, candle light, lamplight, and worst of all by moonlight, it becomes bars! The outside pattern I mean, and the woman behind it is as plain as can be.

I didn't realize for a long time what the thing was that showed behind, that dim sub-pattern, but now I am quite sure it is a woman.

By daylight she is subdued, quiet. I fancy it is the pattern that keeps her so still. It is so puzzling. It keeps me quiet by the hour.

I lie down ever so much now. John says it is good for me, and to sleep all I can.

Indeed he started the habit by making me lie down for an hour after each meal.

It is a very bad habit I am convinced, for you see I don't sleep.

And that cultivates deceit, for I don't tell them I'm awake—O no!

The fact is I am getting a little afraid of John.

He seems very queer sometimes, and even Jennie has an inexplicable look.

It strikes me occasionally, just as a scientific hypothesis,—that perhaps it is the paper!

I have watched John when he did not know I was looking, and come into the room suddenly on the most innocent excuses, and I've caught him several times *looking at the paper!* And Jennie too. I caught Jennie with her hand on it once.

She didn't know I was in the room, and when I asked her in a quiet, a very quiet voice, with the most restrained manner possible, what she was doing with the paper—she turned around as if she had been caught stealing, and looked quite angry—asked me why I should frighten her so!

Then she said that the paper stained everything it touched, that she had found yellow smooches on all my clothes and John's, and she wished we would be more careful!

Did not that sound innocent? But I know she was studying that pattern, and I am determined that nobody shall find it out but myself!

———

Life is very much more exciting now than   sed to be. You see I have something more to expect, to look forward to, to watch. I really do eat better, and am more quiet than I was.

John is so pleased to see me improve! He laughed a little the other day, and said I seemed to be flourishing in spite of my wall-paper.

I turned it off with a laugh. I had no intention of telling him it was *because* of the wall-paper—he would make fun of me. He might even want to take me away.

I don't want to leave now until I have found it out. There is a week more, and I think that will be enough.

I'm feeling ever so much better! I don't sleep much at night, for it is so interesting to watch developments; but I sleep a good deal in the day-time.

In the daytime it is tiresome and perplexing.

There are always new shoots on the fungus, and new shades of yellow all over it. I cannot keep count of them, though I have tried conscientiously.

It is the strangest yellow, that wall-paper! It makes me think of all the yellow things I ever saw—not beautiful ones like buttercups, but old foul, bad yellow things.

But there is something else about that paper—the smell! I noticed it the moment we came into the room, but with so much air and sun it was not bad. Now we have had a week of fog and rain, and whether the windows are open or not, the smell is here.

It creeps all over the house.

I find it hovering in the dining-room, skulking in the parlor, hiding in the hall, lying in wait for me on the stairs.

It gets into my hair.

Even when I go to ride, if I turn my head suddenly and surprise it—there is that smell!

Such a peculiar odor, too! I have spent hours in trying to analyze it, to find what it smelled like.

It is not bad—at first, and very gentle, but quite the subtlest, most enduring odor I ever met.

In this damp weather it is awful, I wake up ˙ he night and find it hanging over me.

It used to disturb me at first. I thought seriously of burning the house—to reach the smell.

But now I am used to it. The only thing I can think of that it is like is the *color* of the paper! A yellow smell.

There is a very funny mark on this wall, low down, near the mop-board. A streak that runs round the room. It goes behind every piece of furniture, except the bed, a long, straight, even *smooch,* as if it had been rubbed over and over.

I wonder how it was done and who did it, and what they did it for. Round and round and round—round and round and round—it makes me dizzy!

———

I really have discovered something at last.

Through watching so much at night, when it changes so, I have finally found out.

The front pattern *does* move—and no wonder! The woman behind shakes it!

Sometimes I think there are a great many women behind, and sometimes only one, and she crawls around fast, and her crawling shakes it all over.

Then in the very bright spots she keeps still, and in the very shady spots she just takes hold of the bars and shakes them hard.

And she is all the time trying to climb through. But nobody could climb through that pattern—it strangles so; I think that is why it has so many heads.

They get through, and then the pattern strangles them off and turns them upside down, and makes their eyes white!

If those heads were covered or taken off it would not be half so bad.

———

I think that woman gets out in the daytime!

And I'll tell you why—privately—I've seen her!

I can see her out of every one of my windows!

It is the same woman, I know, for she is always creeping, and most women do not creep by daylight.

I see her on that long road under the   es, creeping along, and when a carriage comes she hides under th   ackberry vines.

I don't blame her a bit. It must be very humiliating to be caught creeping by daylight!

I always lock the door when I creep by daylight. I can't do it at night, for I know John would suspect something at once.

And John is so queer now, that I don't want to irritate him. I wish he would take another room! Besides, I don't want anybody to get that woman out at night but myself.

I often wonder if I could see her out of all the windows at once.

But, turn as fast as I can, I can only see out of one at one time.

And though I always see her, she *may* be able to creep faster than I can turn!

I have watched her sometimes away off in the open country, creeping as fast as a cloud shadow in a high wind.

—

If only that top pattern could be gotten off from the under one! I mean to try it, little by little.

I have found out another funny thing, but I shan't tell it this time! It does not do to trust people too much.

There are only two more days to get this paper off, and I believe John is beginning to notice. I don't like the look in his eyes.

And I heard him ask Jennie a lot of professional questions about me. She had a very good report to give.

She said I slept a good deal in the daytime.

John knows I don't sleep very well at night, for all I'm so quiet!

He asked me all sorts of questions, too, and pretended to be very loving and kind.

As if I couldn't see through him!

Still, I don't wonder he acts so, sleeping under this paper for three months.

It only interests me, but I feel sure John and Jennie are secretly affected by it.

—

Hurrah! This is the last day, but it is enough. John to stay in town over night, and won't be out until this evening.

Jennie wanted to sleep with me—the sly thing! but I told her I should undoubtedly rest better for a night all alone.

That was clever, for really I wasn't alone a bit! As soon as it was moonlight and that poor thing began to crawl and shake the pattern, I got up and ran to help her.

I pulled and she shook, I shook and she pulled, and before morning we had peeled off yards of that paper.

A strip about as high as my head and half around the room.

And then when the sun came and that awful pattern began to laugh at me, I declared I would finish it to-day!

We go away to-morrow, and they are moving all my furniture down again to leave things as they were before.

Jennie looked at the wall in amazement, but I told her merrily that I did it out of pure spite at the vicious thing.

She laughed and said she wouldn't mind doing it herself, but I must not get tired.

How she betrayed herself that time!

But I am here, and no person touches this paper but me,—not *alive!*

She tried to get me out of the room—it was too patent! But I said it was so quiet and empty and clean now that I believed I would lie down again and sleep all I could; and not to wake me even for dinner—I would call when I woke.

So now she is gone, and the servants are gone, and the things are gone, and there is nothing left but that great bedstead nailed down, with the canvas mattress we found on it.

We shall sleep downstairs to-night, and take the boat home to-morrow.

I quite enjoy the room, now it is bare again.

How those children did tear about here!

This bedstead is fairly gnawed!

But I must get to work.

I have locked the door and thrown the key down into the front path.

I don't want to go out, and I don't want to have anybody come in, till John comes.

I want to astonish him.

I've got a rope up here that even Jennie did not find. If that woman does get out, and tries to get away, I can ti   r!

But I forgot I could not reach far withc   nything to stand on!

This bed will *not* move!

I tried to lift and push it until I was lame, and then I got so angry I bit off a little piece at one corner—but it hurt my teeth.

Then I peeled off all the paper I could reach standing on the floor. It sticks horribly and the pattern just enjoys it! All those strangled heads and bulbous eyes and waddling fungus growths just shriek with derision!

I am getting angry enough to do something desperate. To jump out of the window would be admirable exercise, but the bars are too strong even to try.

Besides I wouldn't do it. Of course not. I know well enough that a step like that is improper and might be misconstrued.

I don't like to *look* out of the windows even—there are so many of those creeping women, and they creep so fast.

I wonder if they all come out of that wall-paper as I did?

But I am securely fastened now by my well-hidden rope—you don't get *me* out in the road there!

I suppose I shall have to get back behind the pattern when it comes night, and that is hard!

It is so pleasant to be out in this great room and creep around as I please!

I don't want to go outside. I won't, even if Jennie asks me to.

For outside you have to creep on the ground, and everything is green instead of yellow.

But here I can creep smoothly on the floor, and my shoulder just fits in that long smooch around the wall, so I cannot lose my way.

Why there's John at the door!

It is no use, young man, you can't open it!

How he does call and pound!

Now he's crying for an axe.

It would be a shame to break down that beautiful door!

"John dear!" said I in the gentlest voice, "the key is down by the front steps, under a plantain leaf!"

That silenced him for a few moments.

Then he said—very quietly indeed, "Open the door, my darling!"

"I can't," said I. "The key is down by the front door under a plantain leaf!"

And then I said it again, several times, very gently and slowly, and said it so often that he had to go and see, and he got it of course, and came in. He stopped short by the door.

"What is the matter?" he cried. "For God's sake, what are you doing!"

I kept on creeping just the same, but I looked at him over my shoulder.

"I've got out at last," said I, "in spite of you and Jane. And I've pulled off most of the paper, so you can't put me back!"

Now why should that man have fainted? But he did, and right across my path by the wall, so that I had to creep over him every time!

"The Confessions of a Nervous Woman"

Anonymous

1896

In an effort to offer insight to the medical establishment, an anonymous patient related her personal struggle against "nervous depression" in the academic journal The Post-Graduate. *The story details her vain attempts to find a cure for her frequent headaches, nervousness, and other symptoms, which she describes in intimate detail. With utter resignation, she perpetuates the prevailing attitudes toward mental illness during the late nineteenth century. "I had a feeling, which many women I know also have, that the womb is the weak point and is the cause of most of their nervous ills," she writes. Her psychological discomfort leads her, as she explains in this narrative, on an "Odyssey" to thirteen doctors.*

I suppose I was always rather nervous. When I was a girl I was easily frightened. I didn't like thunderstorms or cows. I jumped at noises, and at night I had often terrifying dreams. Young men interested me when I grew older, but I didn't like to go into society, though I enjoyed myself when there. My mother had always to urge me to go out.

I was, I can say, bright, alert and usually very good company, but after a day's enjoyment, I would go to bed alm   collapsed, often suffering from a headache that laid me up for one   two days.

My sickness came on rather late—at fifteen—(you say I must tell you all) and I had much pain with it. When I was eighteen I had a hard winter, practicing at the piano, dancing, studying. In the spring I began to have pains in the back, and at times frightful headaches. I was especially sorry, for I had gotten attached to a young gentleman, who was beginning the law in my town. Perhaps he called too often and late. But I at last had a regular attack of what the doctors called nervous prostration or spinal irritation. At any rate, I lay in bed for many months and suffered as women do—from backaches and headaches, and pains boring into the base of my brain.

My doctor tried all kinds of things, but still I was no better. It was then I began to suffer so from noises, even the slightest. The slam of a door gave me agony. At last it was decided that I had some womb trouble, and must be examined. I had some leucorrhœa and pain at my periods, and walking hurt me and tired me so. I can't describe the shock I felt at having to be treated. But my pain was bad and my desire to get well great; besides, I had a feeling, which many women I know also have, that the womb is the weak point and is the cause of most of their nervous ills. Well, I got no better and treatment ceased. As the summer and fall passed I got stronger, though I still had my headaches and was nervous and easily tired. Still I got about and began to join in my former pursuits.

I am not going to weary you with my courtship and marriage. My husband was a fine young man, engaged in business; he was much in love, and so was I.

In the two years after marriage I had two miscarriages. I am not going to deny that I was not one of the many "women who wouldn't." My husband was not rich, and we had moved to the city, and we were happy enough with each other. Besides, I wasn't strong, even directly after marriage. By and by I began to surprise my husband with my nervousness and irritability. I was naturally of a happy and good-natured temperament; but I could no longer bear little things which should have annoyed no one. Mr. L. learned much, I fear, of woman's ways in the first years of his married life. After a time, he began to grow impatient at my frequent headache and backaches and my easily-flowing tears. Still, when I was very   , he was always kind. After a year and a half, however, he and I became convinced something must be done. We were not happy, and I was not well. I couldn't sleep, my headaches increased, a little effort exhausted me, I disliked to go anywhere or do anything, though I did try my best.

Then I began to go to doctors. I have told you something of what you called my medical Odyssey. First I went to an eye doctor. I had in years before tried the usefulness of treating the womb. I was told that my headache and most of my nervousness came from the eyes. I had several different glasses, then my eye muscles were cut. After this I felt better for nearly two months, but I was soon as bad as ever. Another operation and a third did no good and my husband began to complain of doctors' bills, so I stopped. But one day, I got into discussion with my husband and became hysterical, the matter ending in tears and in a long sick headache. So I was taken to a general practitioner. He gave me some tonics and good advice, and I was just about the same. I looked well with the fresh color of my girlhood. I was able to act as though I was not suffering and was often vivacious and apparently happy; but I never was quite unconscious of a headache or a nervous feeling which I can't describe, but which was worse than pain. For some months I had a "fixed idea," as you call it. I had been brought up religiously and I was, I believe, a conscientious girl, trying really to do my best. One day, a gossiping friend told me of a lady who had done something which I had done and who had afterwards become insane. It was a terrible shock to me. I went home and began to brood. I couldn't sleep, I was unhappy almost to desperation, thoughts of suicide even came over me. At first I had a profuse flow of urine, very light colored (you ask for all the details), then a looseness of the bowels; my appetite was gone, I lost flesh and my head was often heavy and confused. The "fixed idea" was always with me. I could not help crying, too, nightly when my husband was away, though I put on as good a face as I could. Finally I told him my trouble. He laughed and made light of it, as I know he had a right to do, for the matter was really not a serious one. But I got no better, and at last he became alarmed and took me to a doctor. This time it was a very eminent gynecologist. He examined me, encouraged me with assuranc   of cure, but said I needed to have an operation done.

I was ready to submit to anything and he "curetted"—that is the word—my womb. Instead of being better, I was a thousand times worse. The shock and pain, or something, increased my nervous depression, and I had, in addition, physical pain in back and head, and I walked with difficulty, becoming tired after a few minutes. I dragged along in this way for several months, and then I went to another gyne-cologist. He told me the operation had not been needed—which was, as you say, easy to determine then. He advised me to call in a general consultant, and I did. The two gentlemen advised me to stop doctor-ing altogether, to rest, live quietly in the country, where I could be out doors and pay no attention to my "idea" or my nervousness.

I did so, and gradually improved. At least, I lost my depression and got stronger.

I was now twenty-five. I had been married five years. My husband had of late had to travel a good deal, leaving me alone. I did not suf-fer, as some women do, for I could amuse myself with music and read-ing, and the companionship of friends. But I did not get strong. I could not sleep well; my stomach, too, was uncertain. Often I had dyspepsia and a persistent pain in the side or over the ovaries. You ask me if I had a displaced kidney, or bowel, or stomach. I don't think that was investigated, but I know that standing or walking brought on pain in the back and often in the bowels as well. Finally I again went to a gynecologist—this time a woman. I went through the always to me distressing ordeal of applications, tampons, etc. It helped me a little, but not much, and I went, after an interval, to another doctor. After he had tried awhile, he sent me to an oculist, for my eyes began to trou-ble me. I couldn't read a page without getting a pain in the back of my head and sometimes in my eyes. The oculist told me my eyes were all right, however, and refused even to prescribe glasses—for which I thank him; I wouldn't like to wear glasses. I haven't lost all my interest in womanly things, and I like still to think I have some of my good looks.

My poor husband was, meanwhile, getting desperate. He had never heard of nerves, and not much of sickness, before his marriage; and I do not much blame him for neglecting me   mes, and at times drink-ing a little. At least, I think now that I do   , but this didn't make my life easier then. Pray, don't suppose I was all the time in tears and hys-terics. Often I could be happy and bright, and sometimes almost for-get myself. Many friends did not even know I was an invalid, or suspect the skeleton in our domestic household. There was no trouble in our conjugal relations. You must know, as well as I, that married women gain many secrets and that there are trouble and nervousness and all that from things that did not affect me. If it is all explained in a popular novel, called "Jude the Obscure," as I am told, I don't want to read it. There is enough unhappiness just from sick headaches and weak nerves and insomnia and neuralgic backs.

When I was twenty-six, another crisis occurred, and I consulted another doctor, who sent me to a sanitarium. There I had all the machinery of a well-equipped institution turned upon me; baths, massage, tamponing, electricity. I was treated earnestly and I am sure intelligently, so far as the doctors knew, and I got some better. But I didn't get well, and after seven months I went home "improved." Since then I have been up and down, but mostly down, and still I have my nerves and my backaches, and I can't do much in any way. I am not like other and healthy women whom I envy so intensely. Here, then, is my story. I am thirty, I have had thirteen doctors, and my life has been a series of treatments. I do not complain of this. Most of my advisers have, I am sure, done their very best for me. But am I never to get well?

LETTERS

ZELDA FITZGERALD

1940, 1947, 1948, AND UNDATED

A once high-spirited flapper who dazzled party-goers alongside her famous novelist husband, Zelda Fitzgerald began, at the age of thirty, to suffer a long series of mental breakdowns. Already a published author of essays and stories, she continued to write during the time she spent in and out of clinics. In addition to producing a novel that appeared in 1932, Fitzgerald wrote volumes of letters that chronicle not only her mental illness, but also her efforts to find personal fulfillment. In this correspondence, published for the first time, she writes to an unnamed reader about her stay at Highland Hospital in Asheville, North Carolina, to her daughter, Scottie, and to her husband, F. Scott Fitzgerald. At the hospital, Zelda Fitzgerald was largely influenced by Dr. Robert Carroll, who was known for the five-mile walks he prescribed for many of his patients. Although Fitzgerald left Highland in 1940—just months before her husband died—she returned periodically for the next several years. In March 1948, she perished, along with eight other women, in a fire that broke out in the hospital kitchen.

[An unaddressed letter written perhaps t   e hospital upon her release.]

Highland Hospital   *Asheville, N.C., 1940*

Without hope of ever again being able to confront the social order with any further fervent interest, heart-broken, grief-stricken, spiritually mortally sick, I was brought to the mountains. The life that I trailed behind the many chaotic concepts which guided me has indeed become a matter of retrospect.

The hospital dozed in the pale sunshine while people hunted around for other people and things, with which to ameliorate my so painful états. Waiting, the possibility of ultimate survival on earth presented itself with so little to recommend it that I envisage with the deepest reluctance even the possibilities of more promise, of yet another effort. However, the head-nurse reappeared and escorted me to walk with a bit of early spring. It seems that the heavens had been in flower for some time but one couldn't tell without entering the park—under the crab apples and the dogwood in bloom, a clear, washed earth offered its violets. It was at last a place to begin, since life must go on.

That after three years of the most precarious and rigorous of adjustments life should once again have become desirable is a matter of my deepest gratitude to Doctor Carroll. After years of enforced introspection and of an unceasing watchful disciplining of the soul, I am again glad to be eager, and grateful for the inexhaustible interest . . . of keeping alive.

Highland Hospital has by the most thoughtful and gentlest of coercions established again my capacity to unify in purpose my aspirations and the immediate exigencies of life on its most factual terms.

I have grown healthy . . . inhaling the attenuate finesse of frosted pines against the early sky, have steeped my better organism in the lovely romantic eternities of mountain dusks. I don't know what further possibilities could be obtained from my present physical endowment. It's good to feel at the height of one's capacities, physically; and good to feel that one is no longer open to almost any betrayal from the delicate balance between the mind and the emotions that guide one.

The three years in Carolina hold, in retrospect, so many fortuitous moments: gardening in the lushly acetic fragrance under the first pear trees in flower; picnic suppers late by a silver-mirrored river; high moons from a mountain-top dreaming over the twinkling vall   he smell of the openfire from the night spent on Mount Mitchell. There have been idyllic days lost in the autumn sun picking apples for the farm—sagas in the bounty and beauty of the land. . . .

Once more I am grateful to Doctor Carroll for the happy three weeks passed so profitably in the Ringling Art School; for the classic glory of swimming in the morning on a beach in Sarasota. The fragrance of golden-rod high above a ballfield on a white-hot summer noon; the spot of the balls on a tennis-court near the end of summer make a pleasant background for such grateful memories.

It's good to have rendered tangible again the capacity to evaluate, to appreciate and to participate lucidly in so remunerating a world, and for the gracious supervision and the careful guidance that I have received at Highland Hospital. I am, once more, gratefully yours, Zelda Fitzgerald

[Written after Fitzgerald's return to Highland Hospital]

Asheville, N.C., 1947

My dearest Scottie,

Have been on a wondrous sketching expedition all day long; miles back into the hills where the orchards tumble down the rambling lanes and golden-rod turns atomic in the sun. I made a couple of sketches of a beauteously bountiful valley with overwhelming mountains billowing off on heavenly grandeurs, and one more friendly glimpse of the world through an apple tree. This is such a lovely part of the world; it is a blessing that God should have had such good ideas.

My tennis is certainly not of the best (if that is what I came to the hospital for) but I play avidly every day despite my advancing years. The woods here are edging with gold; the asters match the dusks heavy with autumnal glamours and the yellow daisies splinter along the road-beds. It is the most appropriate of all seasons for the mountains and I greatly enjoy walking now; and, in fact, <u>almost anything</u> in this ravishing air.

I miss you constantly and can well understand how work would be the more compelling now that fall is here again and the themes of change and of accomplishment again dominant. When Tim is 3 you can deadicate [*sic*] your resources to teaching him his blocks and colors; meantime, you might as well keep the hours in wl   seems to you a felicitous tempo—

I hope that New York is a murmur of undercurrents of excitement as it usually is in Autumn; that the shops shimmer with new gadgets and that the promissory hush of furs and exotic perfumes pervades the elevators and the lobbies—I pray that your job goes well; that Tim and Jack are fine and that you are flourishing.   —Dearest love, Mamma

[Early spring 1948]

Dearest Scottie,

Time goes on turning itself into spring under the mountain-tops and the hillsides are already green. I urgently long to see the new baby and know that you must be engrossed in the affairs of your increased family.

Here we bat the volleyball through the promissory afternoon and mornings dissolve into their own attributes; there are lots of very pleasing people and I go in to Asheville every now and then to sense the tempo of the traffic and see what new aspirations are engrossing the people; in the shop windows anyway. Asheville is always an arbitrary and attenuate little town a-glitter with the promise of an oasis.

I am having insulin treatment, which is extremely disconcerting. However, it is almost over. I will be most grateful to be leaving.

Please write me what goes on chez-vous. You must be enjoying a bloated pompous sense of family. . .

—With dearest love,
Mamma

[Undated]

Dear Scott,

Nobody knows what day, or time, it is here, in this dreamy world where days lose themselves in nostalgic dusk and twilights prowl the alleys lost in melancholic quest.

[I see] that your birthday passed before I thought to wire you.

Many happy returns of the day; and my deepest . . . gratitude for the many happy times we spent together—though it was long ago.

For a long time I have had little use of the passage of time due to being segregate from life and its problems; now that I am once more in contact with routines and rituals that change, I witness ʝ uch of my generation (those that didn't particularly distinguish themselves) on the verge of irrelevance. For a long time it was as if a great many more than is usual with generations were going to be leaders and brilliant people and move in dynamic traditions; but life itself has become so dramatic and so imperative, that no individual destiny can stand against its deep insistencies—save Hitler, or Mussolini.

So here we all are doing whatever we can about whatever we are able and trying to stay out of jail—while the ego is orienting itself in these forceful worlds of less "free-will." . . . I pray in the name of justice, mercy and the beauties of a better-comprehended era. . . .

Scottie told me that your novel progresses—I am so glad that you are able—and know how much more life has to offer with something you care about to nurture.

The best of good luck for the coming year—thanks for all the nice things you have given me   —Devotedly, Zelda

from

THE SNAKE PIT

MARY JANE WARD

1946

By the time The Snake Pit *was published, Mary Jane Ward had married a statistician, sold two moderately successful novels, and suffered a nervous breakdown. In depicting the vagaries of life in a mental hospital, her third published novel captured an enormous readership as a Book-of-the-Month selection. A woman who had once felt blessed by a ten dollar prize she won for her meatloaf recipe suddenly saw her book about isolation and despair generate an estimated $100,000 in sales during its first month. Reviewers praised the book's haunting, yet whimsical, rendering of the fictional mental patient Virginia Cunningham. "I have seldom read a story so consistently convincing," wrote Lewis Gannett in the New York* Herald Tribune. *"This is Virginia, and, but for the grace of God, it might be you or I." In 1948, a film version of* The Snake Pit *starred Olivia de Havilland.*

"Do you hear voices?" he asked.

You think I am deaf? "Of course," she said. "I hear yours." It was hard to keep on being civil. She was tired and he had been asking questions such a long time, days and days of ˙ redibly naive questions.

Now he was explaining that she misunderstood; he did not mean real voices. Fantastic. He was speaking, he said, of voices that were not real and yet they were voices he expected her to hear. He seemed determined that she should hear them. He was something of a pest, this man, but she could think of no decent way to get rid of him. You could tell he meant well and so you tried to play the game with him, as if with a fanciful child.

"You can make water say anything," she said. That should appeal to the childish fancy that leaped from pebble to pebble, dancing in the sun, giggling in the sparkle.

And now the water rushed from the quiet pool of his voice to a stone-cluttered bed uneasy for fishes. The song of the brook soared to a rapid soprano and his voice was changing him into a small boy. Dreadful. She tried not to look, but at last her eyes turned irresistibly and, with horror, saw him a girl. She had suspected him of magic and now she knew.

For once he was not asking questions; he was letting gibberish flow from his lips and you would have far more difficulty making sense from it than you would have in imagining words from a genuine stream. Suppose it was not he.

She turned her head. He had a peculiar habit of crouching behind you. Was he in the bushes? And just who was he? You met so many people and they came and went before you got them sorted out properly. A moment ago he was here and speaking seriously of voices that were not real voices and you knew he would be sad if he discovered that you did not know his name. Never mind. The sun is the chief thing.

The sunshine was a warm almost hot bath of thick gold. There had been no intermediate period, no saying, But it really is getting warmer. You were freezing and then you were warm. Does it happen that way in New York too? New York has so many things over Chicago; I hate for it to have Chicago's ability to make a twinkling change from winter to summer. Maybe I am back in Chicago.

But no. He asked where I was and how pleased he was when I said New York. He said fine, fine. I said I was in ⁻ icago recently for a visit and he said fine, fine. It was as if he was th   acher and I, the student, had given the correct answer to a complicated problem. Yes, he did not ask for information. He was testing me, though God knows why.

He was gone now, at least he was out of sight, out hunting voices that are not voices, poor man, and on the bench was a young woman. She was a pretty girl. Her light curly hair stuck to her forehead in baby rings and her lashes were thick. She might be beautiful if she was not so pale. If I knew her I would suggest liver; perhaps she hates it as much as I do. Robert likes it. I should fix it for him oftener. I can eat the bacon. I could suggest shots. Expensive, though, and she looks poor. Only a very poor girl would go to a public park in a hoover apron. For that hoover? No, that would be collars.

Dear Emily Post: Is it proper to go out park-sitting in a hoover apron? Answer: This is a custom entirely unknown to me, but if it is the general practice in your community it would be well not to be conspicuous. I assume the hoover apron is always fresh and that you would not lap the clean side over the soiled side and attempt in that way to maintain a false front.

Complacently enjoying her advice column in the *Virginia Quarterly,* the *Virginia-Drawn-and-Quarterlied,* Virginia-the-wit looked down at her own garment. Not this old rag. Virginia Stuart Cunningham, Mrs. Robert P. Cunningham to you and Miss Stuart to a minute section of the reading public—the section of literary persons who get their books free.... This young writer from the very proper and intelligent city of Evanston, Illinois, where intelligence is second to nothing but propriety.... Look, Ginger, you wouldn't wear this old thing out to the park, even a New York park.

What was I thinking when I dashed out? I must have been in a rush, but then why sit in the sun? She wore this wreck of a dress only when doing the most revolting of household tasks and she certainly had learned by now that you cannot go out on New York streets looking any old way. You were always running into someone from Evanston. Funny how you could go down to the Loop at home and never see a soul but just step out of your New York apartment and the city swarmed with Evanstonians done up in their most proper and intelligent costumes.

However, the fair girl on the bench was n   n Evanston person. She was not anyone you had ever seen before. You had not been introduced, but she appeared to be talking to you. This city full of people who talked to you at the drop of a hat knocked your hat off. Even so, Virginia Stuart Cunningham was not the type to pick up strangers in the park. Oh, these New York parks. What next?

Yesterday or the day before, I saw a cat on a leash. He was walking along as sedately as a Doberman. Probably they had not let him know he was a cat. Like Margaret. Margaret, when I called kittykittykitty. . . . "Stop that, Virginia," she said. "He doesn't know he's a cat." And the day of the cat on the leash there was a dog in a little plaid coat and he had a plaid cap like Sherlock Holmes' and he was carrying a pipe in his mouth. They had not got him to smoke it, though. Good for him. And good for Mag's cat. That one not only caught on to being a cat, he also had kittens. And Mag always so careful to call him He and she even named him Coolidge. After the kittens Robert said she should have taught him to choose to run. Family fun, not funny to anyone but family. I've seen them all recently. No reason to feel this way. Think about that pipe-carrying dog or you'll begin to bellow.

The poor beast hung its head but marching behind him in oozing pride were a man and woman. . . . No dogs in this park. You wouldn't know you were in New York, the place all bad dogs go when they die. And spend eternity wearing damnfool coats and caps and carrying pipes.

She stirred her shoetips in the dust that lay thick on the path and secretly, not to disturb Miss Hoover, began to look for her groceries and her pocketbook. It was possible that she had not gone to the store yet but not possible that she had come away from home without her purse.

Her eyes were acting up. From the sun. The park might be familiar but the sun flattened the colors and blurred the shapes. It was as if she hadn't her glasses on.

She put her hands up to her eyes and her glasses were not there. "Is there any danger of her ever losing her sight?" Mother asked the doctor. You were ten then. "Well," said the old coot of a doctor, "well, I don't—think so." For years you felt as if you were committing a crime when you read anything that was not Required. And reading was the only thing you cared much for. Well, softball. Yes. What ever became of all those kids, I wonder. Let me see . . . David is a priest, Fred runs a laundry, Kate teaches school . . . Did Edgar end up in jail? Mother said he would. He was a good ball player, though. So was I, in spite of the bum eyes.

Then as you grew older the lenses were changed less frequently and now that you had reached a great age you bought new lenses simply because the old ones had become scratched. Somewhere you read about the possibility of the middle-age farsight correcting the youthful nearsight. Then you are not middle-aged, dearie; still you can't see a foot in front of your face. What are you doing going around without your glasses? Trying to be pretty?

Didn't wear them much in college. Not at a school where there were four or five girls to each boy. I always had more dates than time, though. From going without glasses? Sitting here on this bench she could think of six girls who never wore glasses and who never had dates, except for the political kind got through fraternity blackmail. It is a fine thing for an almost middle-aged woman to sit in the sun and feel smug about having had a lot of dates in college. Where are my glasses?

Where was her pocketbook? Where—this was the real question that gnawed through the artificial frivolity—where exactly was she? . . .

———

It was hazardous for her to go out alone, even with her glasses. She had learned how to get to Wanamaker's and she could find her way to Bleecker Street where the vegetables were cheap and she seldom went many blocks out of the way to reach the French bakery for baba au rhum, so wonderful, with just a touch of nastiness to make you appreciate the wonder. That nasty taste, said Robert, was rum, but that could not be. The medicinal flavor was something they had not been able to overcome yet. Each time she bought the cake she thought now this time they will have got rid of the bad taste. Robert had another explanation that had to do with water poured from stewed flypaper. Quite fresh, unused flypaper, he insisted. But ᴇ ᴜgh of this. You will have to ask the way home.

She hoped Miss Hoover was not a New Yorker. They never know anything. Oh, they know how to get there themselves but blessed if they can tell you. They take a crack at it in their own language. Remember the time the taxi man took us to Pearl Street when we had so distinctly asked for Pell. They and their pell earrings and their store cheese. Half a pound of American cheese, I said, and the grocer said he hadn't any. Well, what do you call that? I pointed to the cheese he was leaning on. That? he said, why, that's store cheese. . . . A few days later I asked this same wiseacre for cottage cheese and he said he had never heard of it. Standing there practically up to his elbows in it. But no, that was pot cheese. Well, where I come from, I said, they call it cottage cheese. He asked where I came from and I said Evanston, Illinois, and he said he had never heard of it and then I betrayed the Athens of the Middle West and said it is a suburb of Chicago. You musta been glad to get away from them gangsters, he said. And when I got home and opened up the carton of cheese it was less than three-quarters full.

If she would just stop talking a minute. A New Yorker, all right, this Miss Hoover. Can't understand a word she says. Pardon me, but could you tell me how to get to . . . ?

How to get to where? Where?

The sun is too warm. Am I going to throw up? Where is the apartment? We have lived so many places. Robert and I. The family and I. After Margaret was born we didn't move so often, but there have been many many places for Robert and me. He lived in the same house all his life until he married.

Since they had been in New York she and Robert had lived in three or four or four or five places. She could say exactly if she put her mind to it. Maybe it was six. It was not that she did not know, it was the sun. She would be able to say their present address as soon as she recovered from this touch of nausea. Even the most familiar things can slip from your head momentarily. You always know where you live. Once some-one telephoned Mother and asked her address and Mother said, "Ex-cuse me a moment, but there's something on the stove." She went to the front porch and read the house numbe   d came back to the tele-phone and said, "There. Now what was i   u wanted?" Yes, anyone could forget his address for an instant. Nothing to get excited about, but it would be convenient to have the front porch along—and your glasses to read the number. But my glasses are here somewhere. A per-son who puts glasses on before getting out of bed is not likely to leave the house without them.

Maybe I am waiting for Robert. He has told me to wait. I almost remember him saying, Now you wait here and I'll be right back.

She pushed her hair from her forehead, no baby rings for this hair. Being without glasses made you feel as if your brain could not function. Her thoughts seemed as blurred as her vision. She sat up straight. She must not become ill.

When she lowered her hands she saw that they were trembling. I am afraid. I wonder why. I am terribly, terribly afraid. . . .

———

"Good morning, ladies."

Who had got into the room? Stealthily she groped for Robert. I must put my hand over his mouth so he won't speak out. But the bed was narrow and she was alone. The room was dark but she saw pale shapes rising up. One of the shapes said her name and then she remembered that she was not at home. February to August.

"Yes," she said. She got out of the cot, fumbled for the bag under the bed and then put on her shoes.

"Hurry up."

"I am." Always the command to hurry and you hurried nowhere, you arrived nowhere. The shoes were cold and clammy and they squished up and down when you walked. . . .

"Where am I going?"

"For shock. You remember."

Do I? I remember it no more than I remember the house where I was born and the little window. Going for shock. An odd, foreign expression. Sensation seekers go to be shocked; I never heard anyone say go for shock, as if it was a commodity like the morning milk.

Presently she and the guard were the only ones left in the washroom. The guard handed her a gray terrycloth robe. "Put this on," she said. "Put your nightgown back on the hanger. ¯ ¯ rry up."

In the hall the guard turned her over to iother one in blue and white, one who hadn't put on any rouge this morning. Virginia and the pale one went through the large room and they reached the outer corridor in time to trail along with the last of the breakfast ladies, but they did not go into the dining room with the breakfast ladies.

As they turned at a door just beyond the dining room door Virginia noticed a third door. It had gold letters on it. It looked familiar but she was unable to make out the letters. The pale one unlocked the door she had selected and they went into a cement stair-well and started to climb. After several flights the pale one unlocked another door and they went into another brown corridor. The pale one escorted her to a small room and left her there. All of this was done without any comment. Well, I don't feel like talking before I've had my coffee either.

There were wooden benches around the walls of the small room and there were two windows. Virginia tried to open one of the windows and was surprised to find that she could. The window opened down the center to make two slits. They might as well have had bars. It was beginning to get light. The sky had a sick, lemon cast at the horizon.

Three robed women were ushered in. One of them sat down; the other two stood in the center of the room. No one said anything.

After a while a guard came and took one of the robed women away. There was pink in the sky now. The pink was turning to red when another woman was taken away. It was nearly light when Virginia was taken.

She was taken down the hall to a little room and the moment she saw that room she knew she had been shocked previously and that she did not care for another helping. The room smelled like her old electric egg beater and there was a dull red glass eye in the wall. "I think I'll go back downstairs," she said.

"You go right on in," said the guard.

"Good morning, Virginia." This was quite a different voice. It was so pleasant that it was silly. It dripped the sort of cheery good will that is hard to take any morning, especially a ᵣrning when you have a formaldehyde hangover.

"Good morning," said Virginia in a tone which she meant to indicate that she wished not to discuss it further.

There was a high table, like an operating table, and she knew she was supposed to get up on it. She got on it and the woman with the silly voice fussed around her. This woman was in an R.N. uniform and the room had somewhat the appearance of an operating room. I'd forgotten I was to have an operation. You don't eat before an operation, of course. I should have remembered. I wonder what I am being operated on for. What haven't I had removed? I believe I still have my gall bladder.

"Well, Jeannie. And how is Jeannie this morning?"

It was he, the Indefatigable Examiner, come out from the bushes. He was wearing a white coat. He had blue eyes and a hawkish nose and a very slender face and his hair was fair and curly.

"And did you enjoy being outside in the park yesterday?" He said this with a heavy accent that you had never been able to place. It wasn't German, French, Italian or Scandinavian. Polish, perhaps. He began to talk at great rate but you could tell he didn't care if you translated or replied. He and the silly woman were busy with their hands. Evidently it was to be a local anesthetic.

They put a wedge under her back. It was most uncomfortable. It forced her back into an unnatural position. She looked at the dull glass eye that was set into the wall and she knew that soon it would glow and that she would not see the glow. They were going to electrocute her, not operate upon her. Even now the woman was applying a sort of foul-smelling cold paste to your temples. What had you done? You wouldn't have killed anyone and what other crime is there which exacts so severe a penalty? Could they electrocute you for having voted for Norman Thomas? Many people had said the country was going to come to that sort of dictatorship but you hadn't believed it would ever reach this extreme. Dare they kill me without a trial? I demand to see a lawyer. And he—he always talking about hearing voices and never hearing mine . . . He, pretending to be so solicitous of me and not even knowing my name, calling me Jeannie. If I say I demand a lawyer they have to do something. It has to ˙ ₍with habeas corpus, something in the Constitution. But they and r smooth talk, they intend to make a corpus of me—they and their good mornings and how are you.

Now the woman was putting clamps on your head, on the paste-smeared temples and here came another one, another nurse-garbed woman and she leaned on your feet as if in a minute you might rise up from the table and strike the ceiling. Your hands tied down, your legs held down. Three against one and the one entangled in machinery.

She opened her mouth to call for a lawyer and the silly woman thrust a gag into it and said, "Thank you, dear," and the foreign devil with the angelic smile and the beautiful voice gave a conspiratorial nod. Soon it would be over. In a way you were glad.

from

Autobiography of a
Schizophrenic Girl

"RENEE"

1951

This short memoir, written by a girl known only as "Renee," was first released in 1951 by a medical publisher. Since that time, it has emerged as a finely wrought gem in the literature of mental illness, read with equal fervor by both mental health professionals and writers. In writing the foreword to a recent edition of Autobiography of a Schizophrenic Girl, *the author Frank Conroy calls the book "an astonishing tour de force of prose." Conroy also recalls that while working on his own memoir,* Stop-Time, *he "invoked Renee often, holding her in my mind as a nervous traveler might hold a St. Christopher medal in his hand."*

I remember very well the day it happened. We were staying in the country and I had gone for a walk alone as I did now and then. Suddenly, as I was passing the school, I heard a German song; the children were having a singing lesson. I stopped to listen, and at that instant a strange feeling came over me, a feeling hard to analyze but akin to something I was to know too well later—a disturbing sense of unreality. It seemed to me that I no longer recognized the school, it had become as large as a barracks; the singing children were prisoners, compelled to sing. It was as though the school   the children's song were set apart from the rest of the world. At the same time my eye encountered a field of wheat whose limits I could not see. The song of the children imprisoned in the smooth stone school-barracks filled me with such anxiety that I broke into sobs. I ran home to our garden and began to play "to make things seem as they usually were," that is, to return to reality. It was the first appearance of those elements which were always present in later sensations and unreality: illimitable vastness, brilliant light, and the gloss and smoothness of material things. I have no explanation for what happened, or why. But it was during this same period that I learned my father had a mistress and that he made my mother cry. This revelation bowled me over because I had heard my mother say that if my father left her, she would kill herself.

One day we were jumping rope at recess. Two little girls were turning a long rope while two others jumped in from either side to meet and cross over. When it came my turn and I saw my partner jump toward me where we were to meet and cross over, I was seized with panic; I did not recognize her. Though I saw her as she was, still, it was not she. Standing at the other end of the rope, she had seemed smaller, but the nearer we approached each other, the taller she grew, the more she swelled in size.

I cried out, "Stop, Alice, you look like a lion; you frighten me!" At the sound of the fear in my voice which I tried to dissemble under the guise of fooling, the game came to an abrupt halt. The girls looked at me, amazed, and said, "You're silly—Alice, a lion? You don't know what you're talking about."

Then the game began again. Once more my playmate became strangely transformed and, with an excited laugh, once more I cried out, "Stop, Alice, I'm afraid of you; you're a lion!" But actually, I didn't see a lion at all: it was only an attempt to describe the enlarging image of my friend and the fact that I didn't recognize her. Suddenly I saw the resemblance of this phenomenon to my nightmare of "the needle in the hay."

It was a dream that recurred often, especially when I was feverish, and it caused me the most frightful anguish. Later I always associated my unreal perceptions with the dream of ˙ needle.

Here is the dream: A barn, brilliantly ıminated by electricity. The walls painted white, smooth—smooth and shining. In the immensity, a needle—fine, pointed, hard, glittering in the light. The needle in the emptiness filled me with excruciating terror. Then a haystack fills up the emptiness and engulfs the needle. The haystack, small at first, swells and swells and in the center, the needle, endowed with tremendous electrical force, communicates its charge to the hay. The electrical current, the invasion by the hay, and the blinding light combine to augment the fear to a paroxysm of terror and I wake up screaming, "The needle, the needle!"

What happened during the rope game was the same sort of thing: tension, something growing inordinately, and anxiety.

From then on, the recreation period at school was often a source of the unreal feeling. I kept close to the fence as though I were indeed a prisoner and watched the other pupils shouting and running about in the school yard. They looked to me like ants under a bright light. The school building became immense, smooth, unreal, and an inexpressible anguish pressed in on me. I fancied that the people watching us from the street thought all of us were prisoners just as I was a prisoner and I wanted so much to escape. Sometimes I shook the grating as though there were no other way out, like a madman, I thought, who wanted to return to real life.

For the street seemed alive, gay and real, and the people moving there were living and real people, while all that was within the confines of the yard was limitless, unreal, mechanical and without meaning: it was the nightmare of the needle in the hay.

I caught myself in this state only in the yard, never in class. I suffered from it horribly but I did not know how to get free. Play, conversation, reading—nothing seemed able to break the unreal circle that surrounded me.

These crises, far from abating, seemed rather to increase. One day, while I was in the principal's office, suddenly the room became enormous, illuminated by a dreadful electric light that cast false shadows. Everything was exact, smooth, artificial, extremely tense; the chairs and tables seemed models placed here and there. Pupils and teachers were puppets revolving without cause, withou ˙ ˙ective. I recognized nothing, nobody. It was as though reality, atten   d, had slipped away from all these things and these people. Profound dread overwhelmed me, and as though lost, I looked around desperately for help. I heard people talking but I did not grasp the meaning of the words. The voices were metallic, without warmth or color. From time to time, a word detached itself from the rest. It repeated itself over and over in my head, absurd, as though cut off by a knife. And when one of my schoolmates came toward me, I saw her grow larger and larger, like the haystack.

I went to my teacher and said to her, "I am afraid because everyone has a tiny crow's head on his head." She smiled gently at me and answered something I don't remember. But her smile, instead of reassuring me, only increased the anxiety and confusion for I saw her teeth, white and even in the gleam of the light. Remaining all the while like themselves, soon they monopolized my entire vision as if the whole room were nothing but teeth under a remorseless light. Ghastly fear gripped me.

What saved me that day was activity. It was the hour to go to chapel for prayer, and like the other children I had to get in line. To move, to change the scene, to do something definite and customary, helped a great deal. Nevertheless, I took the unreal state to chapel with me, though to a lesser degree. That evening I was completely exhausted.

The remarkable thing was that, when I chanced to return to reality, I thought no more of these terrible moments. I did not forget them, but I did not think of them. And still, they were repeated very frequently, pervading a larger and larger segment of my life. . . .

From the point of view of scholarship, my last year at the elementary school was good enough. I took three prizes, two of them firsts. I seemed to have, then, everything necessary for success in the secondary school. Unfortunately, this was not the case, and the cause lay in the "unreality."

At first I had trouble in adjusting to the schedule and to the new teaching procedure. Then three subjects literally terrified me: singing, drawing, and calisthenics, and I might even add sewing.

It seems that I had a pleasant high soprano voice and the teacher counted on me for solo parts in the chorus ⁻ t he noticed pretty soon that I sang off key, singing sharp or flat as   h as a whole step or two when I wasn't watching. Furthermore, I was unable either to learn solfeggio, to beat the measure or to keep the rhythm.

These lessons aroused an immeasurable anxiety quite disproportionate to the cause. It was the same in drawing. I don't know what happened during the summer vacation, but I seemed to have lost a sense of perspective. So I copied the model from a schoolmate's sketch, thus lending a false perspective from where I sat.

In the gymnasium I didn't understand the commands, confusing left and right. As for the sewing lesson, it was impossible to understand the technique of placing patches or the mysteries of knitting a sock heel. Varied as these subjects were, they presented similar problems, so that more and more, despite my efforts, I lost the feeling of practical things.

In these disturbing circumstances I sensed again the atmosphere of unreality. During class, in the quiet of the work period, I heard the street noises—a trolley passing, people talking, a horse neighing, a horn sounding, each detached, immovable, separated from its source, without meaning. Around me, the other children, heads bent over their work, were robots or puppets, moved by an invisible mechanism. On the platform, the teacher, too, talking, gesticulating, rising to write on the blackboard, was a grotesque jack-in-the-box. And always this ghastly quiet, broken by outside sounds coming from far away, the implacable sun heating the room, the lifeless immobility. An awful terror bound me; I wanted to scream.

On the way to school in the morning at seven-thirty, sometimes the same thing happened. Suddenly the street became infinite, white under the brilliant sun; people ran about like ants on an ant-hill; automobiles circled in all directions aimlessly; in the distance a bell pealed. Then everything seemed to stop, to wait, to hold its breath, in a state of extreme tension, the tension of the needle in the haystack. Something seemed about to occur, some extraordinary catastophe. An overpowering anxiety forced me to stop and wait. Then, without anything having actually changed, again realizing the senseless activity of people and things, I went on my way to school.

Happily for me, I fell ill with pulmonary tuberculosis and had to leave school at once for a mountain sanatorium. There, after a few days of anxiety due to the change, I made a ready adjustment because of the regularity of the life.

The crises of unreality decreased noticeably, to be replaced by states of fervor, of exaltation over nature. I was alone in a small room. To listen to the autumn wind rushing through the woods was my greatest joy. But the shrieking and groaning of the forest treated thus roughly aroused an uneasiness that spoiled the pleasure. I believed the wind blew from the North Pole, traveling over the icy Siberian steppes, moaning and protesting in the forest; it was alive, monstrous, bending everything in its way. Then my room became enormous, disproportionate, the walls smooth and shining, the glaring electric light bathing everything in its blinding brightness. The violence of the wind outside rattling the blinds, the rustling, the strangled sighs of the pine branches bowing under the wind, furnished a striking contrast to the quiet and immobility within. Again the terror mounted to a paroxysm. Desperately I wanted to break the circle of unreality which froze me in the midst of this electric immobility.

When we were not engaged in treatment, I asked a friend to play or to talk to me. But despite the play and the conversation, I could not get back to reality. Everything looked artificial, mechanical, electric. To get rid of it I tried to rouse myself. I laughed, I jumped, I pushed things around, shook them to make them come to life. These were horribly painful moments.

How relieved I was when things remained in their customary framework, when people were alive and normal and especially when I had contact with them!

I came down from the mountain for three months, only to go up again for a full year. It was during this year, the first of January to be exact, that for the first time I felt *real fear*. I should emphasize that the unreality had grown greater and the wind had taken on a specific meaning. On windy days in bad weather I was horribly upset. At night I could not sleep, listening to the wind, sharing its howls, its complaints and despairing cries, and my soul wept and groaned with it. More and more I imagined the wind bore a message for me to divine. But what? I still did not know.

It was New Year's when I first experien   what I called *Fear*. It literally fell on me, how I know not. It was afternoon, the wind was stronger than ever and more mournful. I was in the mood to listen to it, my whole being attuned to it, palpitating, awaiting I know not what. Suddenly Fear, agonizing, boundless Fear, overcame me, not the usual uneasiness of unreality, but real fear, such as one knows at the ap-

proach of danger, of calamity. And the wind, as if to add to the turmoil, soughed its interminable protests, echoing the muffled groans of
the forest.

Fear made me ill; just the same I ran out to visit a friend who was
staying at a nearby sanatorium. To get there, a way led through the
woods, short and well-marked. Becoming lost in the thick fog, I circled
round and round the sanatorium without seeing it, my fear augment-
ing all the while. By and by I realized that the wind inspired this fear;
the trees too, large and black in the mist, but particularly the wind. At
length I grasped the meaning of its message: the frozen wind from the
North Pole wanted to crush the earth, to destroy it. Or perhaps it was
an omen, a sign that the earth was about to be laid waste. This idea tormented me with growing intensity. But I remained unaware of the
basis for the fear which from then on came over me at any moment of
the day.

from

FACES IN THE WATER

JANET FRAME

1961

New Zealand writer Janet Frame draws on her own experiences with mental illness to meticulously depict the shattered existence of an institutionalized woman named Istina Mavet in the novel Faces in the Water. *Frame, the daughter of a railroad engineer and a poet who peddled her work door-to-door, was herself misdiagnosed as a schizophrenic and underwent a succession of shock treatments. It was during one of her hospitalizations that she narrowly escaped a frontal lobotomy when a sympathetic doctor released her after learning she had just won a literary award for her first story collection. Frame's life was featured in the 1991 film* An Angel at My Table, *based on her three-volume autobiography.*

After the doctor performed the last shock treatment of the morning he used to go with Matron Glass and Sister Honey for morning tea in Sister's office where he sat in the best chair brought in from the adjoining room called the "mess-room" where visitors were sometimes received. Dr. Howell drank from the special cup which was tied around the handle with red cotton to distinguish the staff cups from those of the patients, and thus prevent the   :rchange of diseases like boredom loneliness authoritarianism. Dr.   vell was young catarrhal plump pale-faced (we called him *Scone*) short-sighted sympathetic over-worked with his fresh enthusiasm quickly perishing under concentrated stress, like a new plane that is put in a testing chamber simulating the conditions of millions of miles of flying and in a few hours suffers the metal fatigue of years.

The morning tea was followed at eleven o'clock by the ritual of Rounds when, accompanied by the ubiquitous Matron Glass and Sister Honey, both acting as go-betweens interpreters and pickets, Dr. Howell would enter the dayroom where the elderly ladies and those younger but not yet fit for work in the laundry or the sewing room or, higher on the social scale, the Nurses' Home, sat drearily turning over the pages of an old *Illustrated London News* or a *Women's Weekly;* or knitting blanket squares for the lepers; or doing fancywork under the supervision of the newly appointed Occupational Therapist who, it was rumored, much to the dismay of many of the hundred women in Ward Four, was having an affair with Dr. Howell.

"Good morning. How are you today?" the doctor would pause sometimes to inquire, smiling in a friendly manner, but at the same time glancing hastily at his watch and perhaps wondering how in the hour before lunch he could possibly finish his rounds of all the women's wards and get back to his office to deal with correspondence and interviews with demanding puzzled alarmed ashamed relatives.

The patient chosen for conversation with the doctor would become so excited at this rare privilege that she sometimes didn't know what to say or else began a breathless account which was cut short by Matron.

"Now doctor's too busy to listen to that, Marion. You get on with your fancywork."

And in an aside to the doctor the omnipotent Matron would whisper, "She's been rather uncooperative lately. We've put her down for treatment tomorrow."

The doctor would nod absent-mindedly, make a fatuous remark and because of his intelligence immediately realize the fatuity and mentally step back from himself like a salesman who has slighted his own wares. He would point with an increase of ;erness to a tapestry or a ring of lazy-daisy stitch thrust before h ɔy a proud patient. Then, giving a troubled guilty glance around the dayroom, he would retreat for the door while Matron Glass and Sister Honey attended to the mechanics of his exit, unlocking and locking the door and keeping at bay those patients whose need to communicate to a sympathetic listener made them hurry forward in a last attempt to show their tapestry or hurl abuse or greet-and-demand with, Hello Doctor when can I go home?

Sometimes, as if in defiance of Matron Glass and Sister Honey, Dr. Howell chose to isolate himself from them and leave the dayroom by the door which opened on to the spacious tree-filled Ward Four Park; then Matron and Sister would stand looking with accusation at each other and with apprehension as the doctor moved away from them; as spiders might look when a so-carefully-webbed fly with one flick of his wings escapes.

It was the youth of Dr. Howell which appealed to us; the other doctors who did not look after us but who were in charge of the hospital were gray-haired and elderly and hurried in and out of their offices down in front of the building like rats in and out of their hiding places; and they sat, in their work, with the same old chewed solutions littered about them, like nesting material. It was Dr. Howell who tried to spread the interesting news that mental patients were people and therefore might like occasionally to engage in the activities of people. Thus were born "The Evenings" when we played cards—snap, old maid, donkey and euchre; and ludo and snakes and ladders, with prizes awarded and supper afterwards. But where was the extra staff to supervise the activities? Pavlova, the one Social Worker for the entire hospital, valiantly attended a few "social" evenings held for men and women patients in the Ward Four dayroom. She watched people mount ladders and slide down chutes and travel home on the red and blue squares of parcheesi. She too was pleased when the climax of the evening came with the arrival of Dr. Howell in sport coat and soft shoes, with his corn-colored hair slicked down and his undoctorly laugh sounding loud and full. He was like a god; he joined in the games and threw the dice with the aplomb of a god hurling a thunderbolt; he put on the appropriate expression of disn   when he was ordered to slide down a chute, but you could see th   : was a charmer even of bile-green cardboard snakes. And of people. He was Pavlova's god too, we knew that; but no amount of leaping about in her soiled white coat with the few bottom buttons undone could help her to steal Dr. Howell from the occupational therapist. Poor Pavlova! And Poor Noeline, who was waiting for Dr. Howell to propose to her although the only words he had even spoken to her were How are you? Do you know where you are? Do you know why you are here?—phrases which ordinarily would be hard to interpret as evidence of affection. But when you are sick you find in yourself a new field of perception where you make a harvest of interpretations which then provides you with your daily bread, your only food. So that when Dr. Howell finally married the occupational therapist, Noeline was taken to the disturbed ward. She could not understand why the doctor did not need her more than anyone else in the world, why he had betrayed her to marry someone whose only virtue seemed to be the ability to show patients who were not always interested, how to weave scarves and make shadow stitch on muslin. . . .

It is said that when a prisoner is condemned to die all clocks in the neighborhood of the death cell are stopped; as if the removal of the clock will cut off the flow of time and maroon the prisoner on a coast of timelessness where the moments, like breakers, rise and surge near but never touch the shore.

But no death of an oceanographer ever stopped the sea flowing; and a condition of sea is its meeting with the land. And in the death cell time flows in as if all the cuckoo clocks grandfather clocks alarm clocks were striking simultaneously in the ears of the prisoner.

Again and again when I think of Cliffhaven I play the time game, as if I have been condemned to die and the signals have been removed yet I hear them striking in my ears, warning me that nine o'clock, the time of treatment, is approaching and that I must find myself a pair of woolen socks in order that I shall not die. Or it is eleven o'clock and treatment is over and it is the early hours or years of my dream when I was not yet sitting in rainbow puddles in Ward Two Yard or tramping the shorn park inside the tall picket fence with its rusty nails sprouting from the top, their points to the sky.

—

There is no past present or future. Using tenses to divide time is like making chalk marks on water. I do not know if my experiences at Cliffhaven happened years ago, are happening now, or lie in wait for me in what is called the future.

I know that the linen room was very often my sanctuary. I looked through its little dusty window upon the lower park and the lawns and trees and the distant blue strip of sea like sticky paper pasted edge to edge with the sky. I wept and wondered and dreamed the abiding dream of most mental patients—The World, Outside, Freedom; and foretasted too vividly the occasions I most feared—electric shock treatment, being shut in a single room at night, being sent to Ward Two, the disturbed ward. I dreamed of the world because it seemed the accepted thing to do, because I could not bear to face the thought that not all prisoners dream of freedom; the prospect of the world terrified me: a morass of despair violence death with a thin layer of glass spread upon the surface where Love, a tiny crab with pincers and rainbow shell, walked delicately ever sideways but getting nowhere, while the sun—like one of those woolly balls we made at occupational therapy by winding orange wool on a circle of cardboard—rose higher in the sky its tassels dropping with flame threatening every moment to melt the precarious highway of glass. And the people: giant patchworks of color with limbs missing and parts of their mind snipped off to fit them into the outline of the free pattern.

I could not find my way from the dream; I had no means to escape from it; I was like a surgeon who at the moment of a delicate operation finds that his tray of instruments has been stolen, or, worse, twisted into unfamiliar shapes so that only he can realize their unfamiliarity while the team around the table, suspecting nothing, wait for him to make the first incision. How can he explain to them what they cannot understand because it is visible only to him? Dutifully I thought of The World, because I was beyond it—who else will dream of it with longing? And at times I murmured the token phrase to the doctor, "When can I go home?" knowing that home was the place where I least desired to be. There they would watch me for signs of abnormality, like ferrets around a rabbit burrow waiting for the rabbit to appear.

I feared the prospect of a single room. Although all the small rooms were "single" rooms the use of the phrase *single room* served to make a threat more terrifying. During my stay in Ward Four I slept first in the Observation Dormitory and later in the dormitory "down the other end" where the beds had floral bedspreads and where, because of the lack of space, there was an overflow of beds into the corridor. I liked the observation dormitory at night with the night nurse sitting in the armchair brought in from the mess-room, knitting an endless number of cardigans and poring over pull-out pattern supplements in the women's magazines, and snatching a quick nap with her feet up on the fireguard and the fire pleasantly warming her bottom. I liked the ritual of going to bed, with the faithful Mrs. Pilling sending in a tray of hot milk drinks, and one of the patients marching in balancing like a wait-ress a high pile of dun-colored chambers. I liked the beds side by side and the reassurance of other people's soft breathing mingled with the irritation of their snoring and their secret conversations and the tinkle-tinkle and warm smell like a cow byre when they used their chambers in the night. I dreaded that one day Matron Glass hearing that I had been "difficult" or "uncooperative" would address me sharply, "Right. Single room for you, my lady."

Hearing other people threatened so often made me more afraid, and seeing that a patient, in the act of being taken to a single room, al-ways struggled and screamed, made me morbidly curious about what the room contained that, overnight, it could change people who screamed and disobeyed into people who sat, withdrawn, and obeyed listlessly when ordered Dayroom, Dining room, Bed. Yet not all peo-ple changed; and those who did not respond to the four-square shut-tered influence of the room, who could not be taught what Matron Glass or Sister Honey decreed to be "a lesson," were removed to Ward Two.

And Ward Two was my fear. They sent you there if you were "un-cooperative" or if persistent doses of E.S.T. did not produce in you an improvement which was judged largely by your submission and prompt obedience to orders—Dayroom Ladies, Rise Ladies, Bed Ladies.

You learned with earnest dedication to "fit ' " you learned not to cry in company but to smile and pronounce y   self pleased, and to ask from time to time if you could go home, as proof that you were getting better and therefore in no need of being smuggled in the night to Ward Two. You learned the chores, to make your bed with the gov-ernment motto facing the correct way and the corners of the counter-pane neatly angled; to "rub up" the dormitory and the corridor, working the heavy bumper on the piece of torn blanket smeared with skittery yellow polish that distributed its energetic soaking smell from the first day it was fetched with the weekly stores in the basket beside the tins of jam jars of vinegar and the huge blocks of cheese and butter which Mrs. Pilling and Mrs. Everett quarried with a knife specially unlocked from the knife box. You learned the routine, that it "was so," that bath night was Wednesday, but that those who could be trusted to wash further than their wrists were allowed to bathe any night in the large bathroom where the roof soared like in a railway station and three deep tubs lay side by side each with its locked box containing the taps. In small print so that one might mistake it for a railway timetable the list of bathing rules was pasted on the wall. It was an old list, issued at the beginning of the century, and contained fourteen rules which stated, for example, that no patient might take a bath unless an attendant were present, that six inches only of water should be run into the bath, the cold water first, that no brush of any kind should be employed in bathing a patient. . . . So we bathed, one in each bath, without screens, gazing curiously at one another's bodies, at the pendulous bellies and tired breasts, the faded wisps of body hair, the unwieldy and the supple shapes that form to women the nagging and perpetual "withness" of their flesh.

from

THE BELL JAR

SYLVIA PLATH

1963

The month before her suicide in 1963, Sylvia Plath first published The Bell Jar *in Great Britain. She wrote her strongly autobiographical novel under the pseudonym Victoria Lucas, fearing that the work might tarnish her reputation as a poet and embarrass family members whose fictional likenesses could be found within the book. Like* The Bell Jar*'s narrator, Esther Greenwood, Plath worked as a guest editor at a magazine in New York City and experienced a mental breakdown that led to a suicide attempt. In 1971, over the objections of her mother,* The Bell Jar *was published posthumously in the United States.*

Doctor Gordon's waiting room was hushed and beige.

The walls were beige, and the carpets were beige, and the upholstered chairs and sofas were beige. There were no mirrors or pictures, only certificates from different medical schools, with Doctor Gordon's name in Latin, hung about the walls. Pale green loopy ferns and spiked leaves of a much darker green filled the ceramic pots on the end table and the coffee table and the magazine table.

At first I wondered why the room felt so safe. Then I realized it was because there were no windows.

The air-conditioning made me shiver.

I was still wearing Betsy's white blouse and dirndl skirt. They drooped a bit now, as I hadn't washed them in my three weeks at home. The sweaty cotton gave off a sour but friendly smell.

I hadn't washed my hair for three weeks, either.

I hadn't slept for seven nights.

My mother told me I must have slept, it was impossible not to sleep in all that time, but if I slept, it was with my eyes wide open, for I had followed the green, luminous course of the second hand and the minute hand and the hour hand of the bedside clock through their circles and semi-circles, every night for seven nights, without missing a second, or a minute, or an hour.

The reason I hadn't washed my clothes or my hair was because it seemed so silly.

I saw the days of the year stretching ahead like a series of bright, white boxes, and separating one box from another was sleep, like a black shade. Only for me, the long perspective of shades that set off one box from the next had suddenly snapped up, and I could see day after day after day glaring ahead of me like a white, broad, infinitely desolate avenue.

It seemed silly to wash one day when I would only have to wash again the next.

It made me tired just to think of it.

I wanted to do everything once and for all and be through with it.

———

Doctor Gordon twiddled a silver pencil.

"Your mother tells me you are upset."

I curled in the cavernous leather chair and faced Doctor Gordon across an acre of highly polished desk.

Doctor Gordon waited. He tapped his pencil—tap, tap, tap—across the neat green field of his blotter.

His eyelashes were so long and thick they looked artificial. Black plastic reeds fringing two green, glacial pools.

Doctor Gordon's features were so perfect he was almost pretty.

I hated him the minute I walked in throu̇ h the door.

I had imagined a kind, ugly, intuitive ̣ looking up and saying "Ah!" in an encouraging way, as if he could see something I couldn't, and then I would find words to tell him how I was so scared, as if I were being stuffed farther and farther into a black, airless sack with no way out.

Then he would lean back in his chair and match the tips of his fingers together in a little steeple and tell me why I couldn't sleep and why I couldn't read and why I couldn't eat and why everything people did seemed so silly, because they only died in the end.

And then, I thought, he would help me, step by step, to be myself again.

But Doctor Gordon wasn't like that at all. He was young and good-looking, and I could see right away he was conceited.

Doctor Gordon had a photograph on his desk, in a silver frame, that half faced him and half faced my leather chair. It was a family photograph, and it showed a beautiful dark-haired woman, who could have been Doctor Gordon's sister, smiling out over the heads of two blond children.

I think one child was a boy and one was a girl, but it may have been that both children were boys or that both were girls, it is hard to tell when children are so small. I think there was also a dog in the picture, toward the bottom—a kind of airedale or a golden retriever—but it may have only been the pattern in the woman's skirt.

For some reason the photograph made me furious.

I didn't see why it should be turned half toward me unless Doctor Gordon was trying to show me right away that he was married to some glamorous woman and I'd better not get any funny ideas.

Then I thought, how could this Doctor Gordon help me anyway, with a beautiful wife and beautiful children and a beautiful dog haloing him like the angels on a Christmas card?

"Suppose you try and tell me what you think is wrong."

I turned the words over suspiciously, like round, sea-polished pebbles that might suddenly put out a claw and change into something else.

What did I *think* was wrong?

That made it sound as if nothing was *really* ong, I only *thought* it was wrong.

In a dull, flat voice—to show I was not beguiled by his good looks or his family photograph—I told Doctor Gordon about not sleeping and not eating and not reading. I didn't tell him about the handwriting, which bothered me most of all.

That morning I had tried to write a letter to Doreen, down in West

Virginia, asking whether I could come and live with her and maybe get a job at her college waiting on table or something.

But when I took up my pen, my hand made big, jerky letters like those of a child, and the lines sloped down the page from left to right almost diagonally, as if they were loops of string lying on the paper, and someone had come along and blown them askew.

I knew I couldn't send a letter like that, so I tore it up in little pieces and put them in my pocketbook, next to my all-purpose compact, in case the psychiatrist asked to see them.

But of course Doctor Gordon didn't ask to see them, as I hadn't mentioned them, and I began to feel pleased at my cleverness. I thought I only need tell him what I wanted to, and that I could control the picture he had of me by hiding this and revealing that, all the while he thought he was so smart.

The whole time I was talking, Doctor Gordon bent his head as if he were praying, and the only noise apart from the dull, flat voice was the tap, tap, tap of Doctor Gordon's pencil at the same point on the green blotter, like a stalled walking stick.

When I had finished, Doctor Gordon lifted his head.

"Where did you say you went to college?"

Baffled, I told him. I didn't see where college fitted in.

"Ah!" Doctor Gordon leaned back in his chair, staring into the air over my shoulder with a reminiscent smile.

I thought he was going to tell me his diagnosis, and that perhaps I had judged him too hastily and too unkindly. But he only said, "I remember your college well. I was up there, during the war. They had a WAC station, didn't they? Or was it WAVES?"

I said I didn't know.

"Yes, a WAC station, I remember now. I was doctor for the lot, before I was sent overseas. My, they were a pretty bunch of girls."

Doctor Gordon laughed.

Then, in one smooth move, he rose to his feet and strolled toward me round the corner of his desk. I wasn't sure what he meant to do, so I stood up as well.

Doctor Gordon reached for the hand that hung at my right side and shook it.

"See you next week, then."

The full, bosomy elms made a tunnel of shade over the yellow and red brick fronts along Commonwealth Avenue, and a trolley car was threading itself toward Boston down its slim, silver track. I waited for the trolley to pass, then crossed to the gray Chevrolet at the opposite curb.

I could see my mother's face, anxious and sallow as a slice of lemon, peering up at me through the windshield.

"Well, what did he say?"

I pulled the car door shut. It didn't catch. I pushed it out and drew it in again with a dull slam.

"He said he'll see me next week."

My mother sighed.

Doctor Gordon cost twenty-five dollars an hour. . . .

———

"Well, Esther, how do you feel this week?"

Doctor Gordon cradled his pencil like a slim, silver bullet.

"The same."

"The same?" He quirked an eyebrow, as if he didn't believe it.

So I told him again, in the same dull, flat voice, only it was angrier this time, because he seemed so slow to understand, how I hadn't slept for fourteen nights and how I couldn't read or write or swallow very well.

Doctor Gordon seemed unimpressed.

I dug into my pocketbook and found the scraps of my letter to Doreen. I took them out and let them flutter on to Doctor Gordon's immaculate green blotter. They lay there, dumb as daisy petals in a summer meadow.

"What," I said, "do you think of that?"

I thought Doctor Gordon must immediately : how bad the hand-writing was, but he only said, "I think I woul ke to speak to your mother. Do you mind?"

"No." But I didn't like the idea of Doctor Gordon talking to my mother one bit. I thought he might tell her I should be locked up. I picked up every scrap of my letter to Doreen, so Doctor Gordon couldn't piece them together and see I was planning to run away, and walked out of his office without another word.

———

I watched my mother grow smaller and smaller until she disappeared into the door of Doctor Gordon's office building. Then I watched her grow larger and larger as she came back to the car.

"Well?" I could tell she had been crying.

My mother didn't look at me. She started the car.

Then she said, as we glided under the cool, deep-sea shade of the elms, "Doctor Gordon doesn't think you've improved at all. He thinks you should have some shock treatments at his private hospital in Walton."

I felt a sharp stab of curiosity, as if I had just read a terrible newspaper headline about somebody else.

"Does he mean *live* there?"

"No," my mother said, and her chin quivered.

I thought she must be lying.

"You tell me the truth," I said, "or I'll never speak to you again."

"Don't I *al*ways tell you the truth?" my mother said, and burst into tears.

SUICIDE SAVED FROM 7-STORY LEDGE!

> After two hours on a narrow ledge seven stories above a concrete parking lot and gathered crowds, Mr. George Pollucci let himself be helped to safety through a nearby window by Sgt. Will Kilmartin of the Charles Street police force.

I cracked open a peanut from the ten-cent bag I had bought to feed the pigeons, and ate it. It tasted dead, like a bit of old tree bark.

I brought the newspaper close up to my eyes to get a better view of George Pollucci's face, spotlighted like a ⸍ ⸌e-quarter moon against a vague background of brick and black sky ⸍ lt he had something important to tell me, and whatever it was might just be written on his face.

But the smudgy crags of George Pollucci's features melted away as I peered at them, and resolved themselves into a regular pattern of dark and light and medium-gray dots.

The inky-black newspaper paragraph didn't tell why Mr. Pollucci was on the ledge, or what Sgt. Kilmartin did to him when he finally got him in through the window.

The trouble about jumping was that if you didn't pick the right number of stories, you might still be alive when you hit bottom. I thought seven stories must be a safe distance.

I folded the paper and wedged it between the slats of the park bench. It was what my mother called a scandal sheet, full of the local murders and suicides and beatings and robbings, and just about every page had a half-naked lady on it with her breasts surging over the edge of her dress and her legs arranged so you could see to her stocking tops.

I didn't know why I had never bought any of these papers before. They were the only things I could read. The little paragraphs between the pictures ended before the letters had a chance to get cocky and wiggle about. At home, all I ever saw was the *Christian Science Monitor*, which appeared on the doorstep at five o'clock every day but Sunday and treated suicides and sex crimes and airplane crashes as if they didn't happen.

A big white swan full of little children approached my bench, then turned around a bosky islet covered with ducks and paddled back under the dark arch of the bridge. Everything I looked at seemed bright and extremely tiny.

I saw, as if through the keyhole of a door I couldn't open, myself and my younger brother, knee-high and holding rabbit-eared balloons, climb aboard a swanboat and fight for a seat at the edge, over the peanut-shell-paved water. My mouth tasted of cleanness and peppermint. If we were good at the dentist's, my mother always bought us a swanboat ride.

I circled the Public Garden—over the bridge and under the blue-green monuments, past the American flag flow   ed and the entrance where you could have your picture taken i   orange-and-white striped canvas booth for twenty-five cents—reading the names of the trees.

My favorite tree was the Weeping Scholar Tree. I thought it must come from Japan. They understood things of the spirit in Japan.

They disemboweled themselves when anything went wrong.

I tried to imagine how they would go about it. They must have an extremely sharp knife. No, probably two extremely sharp knives. Then they would sit down, cross-legged, a knife in either hand. Then they would cross their hands and point a knife at each side of their stomach. They would have to be naked, or the knife would get stuck in their clothes.

Then in one quick flash, before they had time to think twice, they would jab the knives in and zip them round, one on the upper crescent and one on the lower crescent, making a full circle. Then their stomach skin would come loose, like a plate, and their insides would fall out, and they would die.

It must take a lot of courage to die like that.

My trouble was I hated the sight of blood.

I thought I might stay in the park all night.

The next morning Dodo Conway was driving my mother and me to Walton, and if I was to run away before it was too late, now was the time. I looked in my pocketbook and counted out a dollar bill and seventy-nine cents in dimes and nickels and pennies.

I had no idea how much it would cost to get to Chicago, and I didn't dare go to the bank and draw out all my money, because I thought Doctor Gordon might well have warned the bank clerk to intercept me if I made an obvious move.

Hitchhiking occurred to me, but I had no idea which of all the routes out of Boston led to Chicago. It's easy enough to find directions on a map, but I had very little knowledge of directions when I was smack in the middle of somewhere. Every time I wanted to figure what was east or what was west it seemed to be noon, or cloudy, which was no help at all, or nighttime, and except for the Big Dipper and Cassiopeia's Chair, I was hopeless at stars, a failing which always disheartened Buddy Willard.

I decided to walk to the bus terminal and inquire about the fares to Chicago. Then I might go to the bank and withdraw precisely that amount, which would not cause so much suspicion.

I had just strolled in through the glass doors of the terminal and was browsing over the rack of colored tour leaflets and schedules, when I realized that the bank in my home town would be closed, as it was already mid-afternoon, and I couldn't get any money out till the next day.

My appointment at Walton was for ten o'clock.

At that moment, the loudspeaker crackled into life and started announcing the stops of a bus getting ready to leave in the parking lot outside. The voice on the loudspeaker went bockle bockle bockle, the way they do, so you can't understand a word, and then, in the middle of all the static, I heard a familiar name clear as A on the piano in the middle of all the tuning instruments of an orchestra.

It was a stop two blocks from my house.

I hurried out into the hot, dusty, end-of-July afternoon, sweating and sandy-mouthed, as if late for a difficult interview, and boarded the red bus, whose motor was already running.

I handed my fare to the driver, and silently, on gloved hinges, the door folded shut at my back.

from

THE WOMAN WARRIOR

MAXINE HONG KINGSTON

1976

In The Woman Warrior, *Maxine Hong Kingston re-creates the lush myths and ghost stories that were passed down by her immigrant Chinese mother and other "story-talkers." Kingston, a native Californian, wrote the book, in part, as an exploration of identity and as a testament to the enduring power of the women in her family. The theme of madness recurs throughout* The Woman Warrior *as a haunting curse that is endured within virtually every household. In this excerpt, Kingston's mother, known as Brave Orchid, cares for her mad sister, Moon Orchid.*

Brave Orchid sat on a bench at the Greyhound station to wait for her sister. Her children had not come with her because the bus station was only a five-block walk from the house. Her brown paper shopping bag against her, she dozed under the fluorescent lights until her sister's bus pulled into the terminal. Moon Orchid stood blinking on the stairs, hanging tightly to the railing for old people. Brave Orchid felt the tears break inside her chest for the old feet that stepped one at a time onto the cold Greyhound cement. Her sister's skin hung loose, like a hollowed frog's, as if she had shrunken inside ˙ Her clothes bagged, not fitting sharply anymore. "I'm in disguise," ˸ said. Brave Orchid put her arms around her sister to give her body warmth. She held her hand along the walk home, just as they had held hands when they were girls.

The house was more crowded than ever, though some of the children had gone away to school; the jade trees were inside for the winter. Along walls and on top of tables, jade trees, whose trunks were as thick as ankles, stood stoutly, green now and without the pink skin the sun gave them in the spring.

"I am so afraid," said Moon Orchid.

"There is no one after you," said Brave Orchid. "No Mexicans."

"I saw some in the Greyhound station," said Moon Orchid.

"No. No, those were Filipinos." She held her sister's earlobes and began the healing chant for being unafraid. "There are no Mexicans after you," she said.

"I know. I got away from them by escaping on the bus."

"Yes, you escaped on the bus with the mark of the dog on it."

In the evening, when Moon Orchid seemed quieter, her sister probed into the cause of this trouble.

"What made you think anyone was after you?"

"I heard them talking about me. I snuck up on them and heard them."

"But you don't understand Mexican words."

"They were speaking English."

"You don't understand English words."

"This time, miraculously, I understood. I decoded their speech. I penetrated the words and understood what was happening inside."

Brave Orchid tweaked her sister's ears for hours, chanting her new address to her, telling her how much she loved her and how much her daughter and nephews and nieces loved her, and her brother-in-law loved her. "I won't let anything happen to you. I won't let you travel again. You're home. Stay home. Don't be afraid." Tears fell from Brave Orchid's eyes. She had whisked her sister across the ocean by jet and then made her scurry up and down the Pacific coast, back and forth across Los Angeles. Moon Orchid had misplaced herself, her spirit (her "attention," Brave Orchid called it) scattered all over the world. Brave Orchid held her sister's head as she pul on her earlobe. She would make it up to her. For moments an atte   eness would return to Moon Orchid's face. Brave Orchid rubbed the slender hands, blew on the fingers, tried to stoke up the flickerings. She stayed home from the laundry day after day. She threw out the Thorazine and vitamin B that a doctor in Los Angeles had prescribed. She made Moon Orchid sit in the kitchen sun while she picked over the herbs in cupboards and basement and the fresh plants that grew in the winter garden. Brave

Orchid chose the gentlest plants and made medicines and foods like those they had eaten in their village.

At night she moved from her own bedroom and slept beside Moon Orchid. "Don't be afraid to sleep," she said. "Rest. I'll be here beside you. I'll help your spirit find the place to come back to. I'll call it for you; you go to sleep." Brave Orchid stayed awake watching until dawn.

Moon Orchid still described aloud her nieces' and nephews' doings, but now in a monotone, and she no longer interrupted herself to ask questions. She would not go outside, even into the yard. "Why, she's mad," Brave Orchid's husband said when she was asleep.

Brave Orchid held her hand when she appeared vague. "Don't go away, Little Sister. Don't go any further. Come back to us." If Moon Orchid fell asleep on the sofa, Brave Orchid sat up through the night, sometimes dozing in a chair. When Moon Orchid fell asleep in the middle of the bed, Brave Orchid made a place for herself at the foot. She would anchor her sister to this earth.

But each day Moon Orchid slipped further away. She said that the Mexicans had traced her to this house. That was the day she shut the drapes and blinds and locked the doors. She sidled along the walls to peep outside. Brave Orchid told her husband that he must humor his sister-in-law. It was right to shut the windows; it kept her spirit from leaking away. Then Moon Orchid went about the house turning off the lights like during air raids. The house became gloomy; no air, no light. This was very tricky, the darkness a wide way for going as well as coming back. Sometimes Brave Orchid would switch on the lights, calling her sister's name all the while. Brave Orchid's husband installed an air conditioner.

The children locked themselves up in their bedrooms, in the storeroom and basement, where they turned on the lights. Their aunt would come knocking on the doors and ᵧ, "Are you all right in there?"

"Yes, Aunt, we're all right."

"Beware," she'd warn. "Beware. Turn off your lights so you won't be found. Turn off the lights before they come for us."

The children hung blankets over the cracks in the doorjambs; they stuffed clothes along the bottoms of doors. "Chinese people are very weird," they told one another.

Next Moon Orchid removed all the photographs, except for those of the grandmother and grandfather, from the shelves, dressers, and walls. She gathered up the family albums. "Hide these," she whispered to Brave Orchid. "Hide these. When they find me, I don't want them to trace the rest of the family. They use photographs to trace you." Brave Orchid wrapped the pictures and the albums in flannel. "I'll carry these far away where no one will find us," she said. When Moon Orchid wasn't looking, she put them at the bottom of a storage box in the basement. She piled old clothes and old shoes on top. "If they come for me," Moon Orchid said, "everyone will be safe."

"We're all safe," said Brave Orchid.

The next odd thing Moon Orchid did was to cry whenever anyone left the house. She held on to them, pulled at their clothes, begged them not to go. The children and Brave Orchid's husband had to sneak out. "Don't let them go," pleaded Moon Orchid. "They will never come back."

"They will come back. Wait and see. I promise you. Watch for them. Don't watch for Mexicans. This one will be home at 3:30. This one at 5:00. Remember who left now. You'll see."

"We'll never see that one again," Moon Orchid wept.

At 3:30 Brave Orchid would remind her, "See? It's 3:30; sure enough, here he comes." ("You children come home right after school. Don't you dare stop for a moment. No candy store. No comic book store. Do you hear?")

But Moon Orchid did not remember. "Who is this?" she'd ask. "Are you going to stay with us? Don't go out tonight. Don't leave in the morning."

She whispered to Brave Orchid that the reason the family must not go out was that "they" would take us in airplanes and fly us to Washington, D.C., where they'd turn us into ashes ⁻ ιen they'd drop the ashes in the wind, leaving no evidence.

Brave Orchid saw that all variety had gone from her sister. She was indeed mad. "The difference between mad people and sane people," Brave Orchid explained to the children, "is that sane people have variety when they talk-story. Mad people have only one story that they talk over and over."

Every morning Moon Orchid stood by the front door whispering, whispering. "Don't go. The planes. Ashes. Washington, D.C. Ashes." Then, when a child managed to leave, she said, "That's the last time we'll see him again. They'll get him. They'll turn him into ashes."

And so Brave Orchid gave up. She was housing a mad sister who cursed the mornings for her children, the one in Vietnam too. Their aunt was saying terrible things when they needed blessing. Perhaps Moon Orchid had already left this mad old body, and it was a ghost badmouthing her children. Brave Orchid finally called her niece, who put Moon Orchid in a California state mental asylum. Then Brave Orchid opened up the windows and let the air and light come into the house again. She moved back into the bedroom with her husband. The children took the blankets and sheets down from the doorjambs and came back into the living room.

Brave Orchid visited her sister twice. Moon Orchid was thinner each time, shrunken to bone. But, surprisingly, she was happy and had made up a new story. She pranced like a child. "Oh, Sister, I am so happy here. No one ever leaves. Isn't that wonderful? We are all women here. Come. I want you to meet my daughters." She introduced Brave Orchid to each inmate in the ward—her daughters. She was especially proud of the pregnant ones. "My dear pregnant daughters." She touched the women on the head, straightened collars, tucked blankets. "How are you today, dear daughter?" "And, you know," she said to Brave Orchid, "we understand one another here. We speak the same language, the very same. They understand me, and I understand them." Sure enough, the women smiled back at her and reached out to touch her as she went by. She had a new story, and yet she slipped entirely away, not waking up one morning.

Brave Orchid told her children they must help her keep their father from marrying another woman because she ˙˙ ln't think she could take it any better than her sister had. If he brou₀ another woman into the house, they were to gang up on her and play tricks on her, hit her, and trip her when she was carrying hot oil until she ran away. "I am almost seventy years old," said the father, "and haven't taken a second wife, and don't plan to now." Brave Orchid's daughters decided fiercely that they would never let men be unfaithful to them. All her children made up their minds to major in science or mathematics.

from

THE LOONY-BIN TRIP

KATE MILLETT

1990

Not long after she appeared on the cover of Time *magazine as the author of the feminist manifesto* Sexual Politics, *Kate Millett was committed to psychiatric hospitals, first in California and later in Minnesota. Hurriedly diagnosed as a manic-depressive, Millett suffered the indignity of locked wards and the painful stigma that is all too often associated with mental illness.* The Loony-Bin Trip, *published nearly two decades after her forced hospitalizations in America, recounts Millett's personal odyssey, including a fateful stay at a psychiatric facility in Ireland.*

Tonight big nurse found me out. After the lithium pill was duly given and received (in time the blood count would tell them if their own vigilance had not observed), she noticed. Waited until I swallowed—and then her instinct grabbed for me and found the pill still in my cheek. I could swallow then or confront. I decided to confront. The speech about civil liberties, about forced medication of unexplained substances. Carried away with my case, I demonstrated the tablets in the right-hand pocket of my Mexican shirt. That was it. Swallow or else. "And you are to swallow this, too." "What` ` `?" "Thorazine."

Prescribed, one supposes, since the break(Although here one hardly knows, since pills appear to be meted out with such abandon, especially by the night shift, who have bags of them. Cellophane bags with pills of all colors, doled out at night as delicacies, the older women and the more depressed eager to accept them as tickets to sleep, to dreams—dreams advertised as wonderful by the dispensers.

At times I imagine they are testing drugs for manufacturers or catering to drug addiction as a subterranean way of life here, the night life. The things of the day are not the things of the night here at all, the night staff a different breed, meaner, further inclined to have no contact with the patients. Unlike the maternalistic scolding habits of the day staff, who treat us as defective children, the night staff treat us more like convicted felons.

And now there is a fairly hideous Thorazine syrup I am to consume in the evening. Pretending to myself that it is brandy or Drambuie or some Irish liqueur I haven't come across in the outside world. Drinking it slowly, trying to avoid its odious taste and convert it to booze or pleasure or a treat—anything but punishment to darken the mind. Mixing it with milk or drinking it in alternate drafts while the night nurse bellows that I finish. Defying her, pretending to like it. By God, she forces more upon me. Prescribed? Who knows, by a doctor, by her whim, who knows?

I only know that it will take more oranges to beat it. More coffee if I could get it, or straight black tea. I begin to eat fruit like an athlete. To save it in my dresser, to go through six oranges a day. I begin to thirst. For, of course, Thorazine is thirst. The women talk of another drug here—Prolixin. As for Thorazine, it's not watered down with orange juice as in America. This is straight shots, big shots. What is it? What is it doing to my mind? Thorazine is hallucinatory. I hardly need that while trying to maintain my sanity against this place. But what is Prolixin?

———

I have lost the sense of being the quiet one here, the nearly invisible being at teatime. Only noticed at the very end, then she takes her tablet obediently. Polite, nondescript; even the accent and the foreignness go unnoticed, since she never says a 'ing in the nurses' presence. Out of sight of the guards she is th 'e of the party, amusing and clowning and waking up and occupying the listless, learning their stories, finding out about the place, discovering who is getting shock. Always the battered-looking ones, utterly terrified, who either know it is punishment or try desperately to tell themselves it is for their own good. But in the telling, the truth hits them in the face as they talk.

Mostly they are silent and tremble, their hands a Saint Vitus' dance over the chenille laps of their bathrobes; their faces red, their tongues difficult to control. Other tongues, too: the Thorazine tongues that swell and thirst constantly; most of the day but a quest for liquid of some kind.

Ann's husband put her here, Mary's in-laws, Margaret's own mother. And the visits, even the visits of the culprits, are cherished, awaited, loved, hated, feared. Boredom and necessity together.

If I could get the dope on this place, the drugs and the shock particularly, then Deirdre's friend Charlotte, who is a member of the Irish parliament, could look into it. Just the sight of our peeling paint and the jaundiced walls—the diseased look of the plaster in that corner of the ceiling in the dayroom—would incite a committee.

There has recently been a scandal over Irish loony bins; maybe we could get some mileage out of that. Just "mileage," of course, since what is really wrong, the drug—the drug as healer, as official method now—is insidious, the true evil. Generally the drug is advocated because it pacifies and makes work easy for the aides and nurses, the guards. Actually it does a great deal more, all very contrary to sanity; it induces visions, hallucinations, paranoia, mental confusion. Nothing could be harder than to maintain sanity against the onslaught of a drug. The bin itself is insane, abnormal, a terrifying captivity, an irrational deprivation of every human need—so that maintaining reason within it is an overwhelming struggle. After a certain time many victims collapse and agree to be crazy; they surrender. And withdraw. And as time goes by, they cannot or finally will not return; it is too far, it is too unrewarding, it is too dubious—they have forgotten. And they limit their lives to their own minds, the diversions within them. The woes and gratifications of some carefully wrought fantasy, built like a nest out of the tatters of what was once a life I :ould be no longer.

Odd how the shape of an institution, its inte   n and definition, affect its inmates: felons remain sane in prison, because it is prison and not a loony bin. The very purpose of the bin and what all understand by its meaning predicate madness. To remain sane in a bin is to defy its definition. The general understanding is that one does not get there till crazy and one gets out only when well, that is, cured and purged of craziness. And what is the cure—fear? Is the danger of endless captivity supposed to motivate one into reason? For me it has the opposite effect. The more I am afraid I will never get out, the more anxious I am. The more eager to find a way out, whether it be telephone or mail, friends or a walk to the hotel. And now that escape has failed me I realize I have sunk deeper here, lost points, will be watched as a jumper from now on, drugged harder. I have come to their attention, need closer supervision. Another attempt, and it would be more than your old brown trousers that you'd lose. There must be "quiet" rooms in this passage. There is shock certain mornings.

To keep your mind, assailed here on every side by the place itself, you will have to fight the drugs now. You have defied the guards, drunk their stuff as cheerfully as if it were booze, it will be a game for them now to drug you. Since you are too afraid to sleep at night, the issue of when—if ever—you will get out of here becomes more crushing then. With time alone, you pace back and forth to the bathroom, trying to plan, trying to figure out who, if anyone, could even know you are here. D'arcy, Deirdre, Moira, the women in Dublin. Desmond. If he knows, why doesn't he do something? Why doesn't he tell the others? If Sophie knows . . . and she must—she was on the phone through some amazing conference call at the same time as Desmond and the cops at the airport and that stuffed-shirt doctor. A tailor's dummy with a paper you do not even know if you signed, let alone what it was—scared, rabbit-scared. Now all these days later—how many days?—count, try to remember what day you were busted. They took you right here, installed you that night—the little beard and the good suit. McShane you saw the next day. The next day—how do you remember it and the one after? By what was on television? By counting your packs of cigarettes; you ordered a carton but got only five. Why do they cost twice as much here ˉ ˉ ver mind—do you have enough money in that purse to keep buyiɳ garettes? There is never enough time to count it when they let you have it. Remember to work that out—some of the money is in traveler's checks, or the Bank of Ireland. Fool, you now have a checking account in this country and can't use it; this joint is never going to take checks.

Forget it—who, who could help, come to the rescue? Desmond—I cannot believe this of Desmond: a rebel, a freedom fighter. But a lawyer. Then the women, but do they know? Sophie—would she come all this way? Mallory, having seen the error of her ways? Absurd. There is no help from America then; only Sophie and the family would know and a few friends—who will decide from what they've heard that I'm in exactly the right place and getting wonderful care. The Irish women then—which of them? Whoops, the night nurse. Just finishing, touch of diarrhea. Yes, of course, I'll get right back in bed. No, I'm sure I won't need anything to sleep. No, really. No. And the needle jabs your rear like an insult and the white stupor comes over, fast so fast, and then more of the terrible dreams.

—

The dreams of Prolixin. Like a white club it comes down and for a little while you are unconscious. Then it begins. I am totally conscious, horribly awake and yet rigid, locked in the dream. There is no way out of this fate, the same dream over and over, only worse. More certain. It starts with the back windows of the dormitory, which even in daytime haunt me. As does the skylight, the passage to heaven, the route of the fliers. For in the dream one is tempted first that way, to join the others and take the night flights, the pills taken willingly for those moments of ecstasy when, as in a pre-Raphaelite painting, the old ladies of the ward rush like angels through the skylight and then disperse into the greatest freedom of all, autoflight, da Vinci's aspiration fulfilled in their gray nightclothes escaping through the hatch. And if you give in, if you don't keep working to get out of here, that is how you will go. Up the hatch. Feel the air, the breath of freedom, riding the clouds and winds, witches on their night ride. Don't, don't. Stay on the ground. They buy you with this. But you are already inoculated with the nightmare toxin, so you won't even get off the ground. And you will never get out of here either.

Then the windows onto the trees, the view   the back fields. You will be a face in one of these windows. Years. A face like aging paper—old, then older. Looking out. Mute. Helpless, a cipher without method or manner of communication. Silent, like an illusion. A reminder of hardly anything at all. Just this white figure behind glass over the years. It will beckon less but the face cannot refrain from its appeal, its last gesture no one will ever see. These windows look out only upon a few trees; there is no path there even, only a gardener, the dogs at night. Far away in New York, America, the people she knew will lose count, forget, be told first that she had a medical illness as well, pneumonia perhaps, a broken arm. Months, then half a year, then a year and a half. The doctors reporting but with diminishing punctuality. Friends hearing that the condition is incurable, madness has won; she is best off there. The people in the hospital are kind, she has everything she wants, she loves Ireland. Arrangements will have to be made about the farm. A shaggy mess of neglect and sold for a poor price, but what else can be done? No one has time or inclination to tend the place. And that art colony business was daffy, the sort of deluded scheme that is to be expected in the manic type. Everything was left most untidy. Years ago. Now only this face in the window.

———

You are in the hard lock of Dr. Strong now forever. You are in the hands of the Church you ran away from so long ago, down the stairs out of the confessional onto the streets. The stone arm has you now, those same cut stones. Despite the presence of the state it is finally Rome that has you prisoner. Ironic shiver that it would come to this; that you could evade your heritage this far only to end up here, a cripple and infirm, an aging crone among the nuns, all your little American freedom fighter business quite over, women's lib and other notions crunched like cellophane in the strength of this stone force.

———

Rome barks like the dog at the end of a fairy tale read once upon your father's lap, where the little boy or girl, the quester, enters an underground chamber, and there atop a chest is a great snarling dog. In black and white in the book we read together; he read the words, I read the pictures. The pen-and-ink illustr ˙ ns drawn fierce and terrible. You are there now, descending eve ˍ ang until you reach the last barred door and there is the dog. The Pope. A dog enthroned. Fangs. Alive, buried alive in the stone rooms, the stone corridors, the barred doors, the teeth that guard or bite. That rivet you into a small space underground without air or light. Dark it is now, farther down, and the games begin. Oh God, not the games, not the dials, not the

horrors of the last one. I remember the last dream all over in this one.
The dials like the dials on a gas meter but worse, harder to interpret
and more erratic, inscrutable. The winged skate like a token in Mo-
nopoly. The dials spinning are expenses and then become time and
then become death itself and I watch my death and gasp. If they spun
the other way? But no. Spin spin and the winged skate comes like fate,
a portentous and shining little emblem. In this figure, senseless yet full
of meaning, I study my chances of being freed, of being killed slowly
by years. Still hanging on to hope as it drains away. Spin. Faster the
winged skate. The dials. Finally the last figure, the Pope in hell. He is
there and I am his prisoner in hell. The robes, the miter, the throne. I
hate him utterly in this dream. The Papacy, not even the Pope. Surely
not the jolly TV Pope of the upper regions but the shadow Pope, the
Pope behind the Pope: the historical truth, the figure through the ages,
the Popes of the Inquisition, the holders of hellfire and the stake. And
I am found out. The final laugh. Witch and pretender. A Joan, a
heretic. And they have me now.

I am in their dungeon and their jail. From this room—if you refuse
the skylight and stand your ground, wanting out, wanting the trees
outside and the roads—from this room you will go to another. To solitary, then cell after cell, farther and deeper, until this last game of all,
the dials and the skates. The shiny little Atlantic City figure of a
winged skate, the token in a Cracker Jack box, emblem of some pin-
ball machine, mechanistic allegory of fate. And the ugly little gas
meter dials, like dials in cheap rooms in England where you pay a
penny for a few hours' warmth. They swirl, moving the way electrical
dials swirl around when klieg lights are on; fast, faster. You never know
which dial registers which thing. Just as when the company lets you
read your own dial—since you do not understand it, you cannot cheat
or foreknow—so it is here. And the red figu   of the Pope on his
throne, waiting like a spider below a grating,   n down, dizzy into
hell—they have made me dream this. This is their punishment, their
lesson. Every night I will be tortured thus. And if I resist they will tie
me down to inoculate me with this horror, this eight hours of hellfire.
Exhausted into the gray light of morning.

Waking to our great sad room of waking women, each a prisoner in her mind and body. The heart flutters: perhaps today, surely today, it must be today that there will be news. Word. Desmond. Today they will let me phone. If not phone, then write; a far smaller opportunity, of course—so humble, a stamp and real paper. All that is written on toilet paper, in emulation of Armagh and out of the same necessity, all that is stored up and ready. But for nothing. Not without stamps, not without their permission or someone to pass it to. I cannot keep the letters in my purse, since it is in the possession of the staff. And my little bedside dresser is also unsafe. So, like all the other women here, I have adopted a shopping bag that goes with me everywhere and is guarded all the time from the guards but left about continually among the women. There is nothing to steal; I give my cigarettes away and include sharing them in the ration I count on. But I always know where the bag is when the door opens loudly upon a nurse. Today—something must happen today. I cannot stand more of these nights. In the day I can think, hold on to my mind, resist Thorazine and the other stuff with oranges and milk and bread and hard tea and determination.

But not the nighttime, Prolixin. Asking the other women to repeat the name of it for me and what they know about it, I suddenly remember it is mentioned in the H Blocks book—it is the stuff they force upon the prisoners in northern Ireland. One of the strikers' demands is to stop having Prolixin foisted upon them under the pretext of testing it. "An experimental drug developed in England for use upon schizophrenics." Political punishment, sadistic control. Old women here show me blisters on their backs from the stuff, years of large doses. Something has to happen today. The windows onto the service road, the little car park—there, someone will come from there. Watch for them or they will be turned away. The doctors will say you are resting, better, doing nicely. Must not be disturbed, have requested no visitors.

from

BY HER OWN HAND

SIGNE HAMMER

1991

On a quiet night in a Pennsylvania suburb, nine-year-old Signe Hammer was awakened from her sleep and drawn to the kitchen, where she saw one of her brothers feeling for a pulse on a body. With their father out of town on business, Hammer and her brothers had discovered that their mother had committed suicide. "I disappeared," Hammer wrote as an adult. "What I have been trying to find out all these years is, where did I disappear to?" In this excerpt from her memoir By Her Own Hand, *Hammer revisits the event that so profoundly shaped her identity.*

I'm very young, my first time at the theater. Mary Poppins has taken the Banks children to tea at the home of some friends of hers, and while they sit on the late-Victorian furniture it rises, gently, toward the ceiling. The Banks children's eyes bug out, my eyes bug out, the production is a hit. And they eat real fruitcake.

I know the fruitcake is real because we go onstage afterward and I take a good look at it. It immediately suggests to me the possibility of a whole life onstage, where everyone could see me but I would be set off from them, in a magical space where I coul᾽ ᾽rform magical acts, like flying. Yet I could eat real fruitcake. The i   e dazzles.

At home I immediately start to draw pictures for plays, hanging the pictures up on my little red wooden wheelbarrow and delivering the narration, like a slide show. As soon as I learn to write, I become the school playwright and star performer. At will I can change my geography, my time, my family, my age, my sex.

When I was nine, though, something happened that put an end to this activity. In the spring of 1950, right before Easter, resurrection time, my mother decided to go in the other direction. She committed suicide.

Her method was simple and effective. One night, when my father was away and we children had gone to bed, she set up the ironing board in front of the open oven, turned on the gas, lay down on the ironing board, and waited for the gas to do its work.

I don't know how she got herself onto the ironing board; she was five-foot-six or so, according to one photograph I have in which she is posed in front of a measuring scale, probably for an army PX I.D. I don't actually remember the ironing board; it is a detail supplied by one of my brothers, in the only conversation we ever had about our mother's death. We were adults by then, and he had had a few drinks, so I suppose it is the truth.

At some point after she lay down, and probably after she died, there was an explosion; she had forgotten, apparently, to turn off the refrigerator, and some spark ignited the gas. Or was that part of her plan, to dispose of the gas so none of us would be overcome by it when we found her?

She hadn't wanted to take me with her. My room, tiny and high-ceilinged, was right above the kitchen, in the back of the house. There was an old-fashioned iron grill in the floor to allow warm kitchen air to flow through. It had been covered over because I couldn't sleep with people down there clattering dishes and arguing, but she must have wanted to make sure. So when it was time to go to bed she asked me whether, as a treat, I wanted to sleep in the guest room, in the front of the house next to the room she shared with my father.

She knew I would accept. I hated my room, set apart from everyone else's. My three brothers slept in a cluster bedrooms on the third floor that we called the boys' dormitory. I d been a few years since I had been so frightened by my nighttime isolation that I had braved the black wells of the back and front stairs to get to the safety of my parents' bed, but I still loved sleeping in the guest room. It felt like I belonged somewhere, with people.

When she came to tuck me in that night she hugged me long and hard, wrapping her arms around my shoulders and lifting me up to her. She held me as if she were reminding herself of what it felt like. When she went back downstairs, she left the door open a few inches so I could see the light from the hall.

The explosion hit my sleep as a sentence in a dream: "The books fell on the floor." I woke up hearing my brothers pounding down the back stairs, caught a glimpse of flying pajamas. I went wide-eyed next door, and saw that the bed was still made, as if it were daytime. I knew something was all wrong, and followed my brothers down to the kitchen.

Erik was out in the driveway yelling FIRE!, his voice cracking a little in panic. Hal was in the kitchen, standing over my mother, feeling for a pulse. She was dressed in her old brown house slacks and a red sweater.

I walked several hesitant steps into the kitchen, over ash that had been paint, seared from the ceiling and cabinets. I noticed a little blue line of flame along the wooden counter. That must have been the moment I knew my mother was dead, because I stopped, backed up, and stood in the doorway, unable to move.

—

A dead body is like a black hole in space; it sucks everything in and gives nothing back. You can't take your eyes off it, because you can't believe it's not going to move. But it denies you; it's absent.

I had seen death once before. The death I knew was that of a cat, curled up in its usual place on a bit of carpet at the foot of the cellar stairs. It, too, looked stiff, angular; the form of cat was there, but the thing that had made it cat was gone. It had become like an old dustcloth rinsed, wrung out, and left to dry to a stiff twist. I thought it could happen to me, anytime.

We buried the cat in a cardboard box in ˙ dirt by the kitchen foundation wall, where my mother grew a few ʀ bushes. Afterward I felt cut off from myself. The cat's death short-circuited the connection that had gone through its juicy little body, its purr, its soft fur, that were all something like love. I resented this disconnection, but I felt a panicky helplessness, too.

The cat and my mother had become untouchable.

———

After a while, neighbors appeared, and I was sent upstairs to my own room, to grope in the smoke for my bathrobe. Nobody thought it was strange to send me on this errand; it was a reflex, to behave as though nothing had happened. I worried about my hamster in his cage in the basement, but I was not allowed to go down and get him. Nobody hugged me; nobody hugged anyone, then or later. (As far as I know, the only one who ever mourned, besides myself, was my father: Not long afterward, I heard him roaring through the empty rooms of the first house we moved to after the suicide, bellowing AGNES! at the top of his lungs. He thought he was alone, but I was sitting on a little bench in the kitchen entryway, just outside the screen door, and I heard. I didn't recognize my father; his grief was terrifying. He never knew that I knew; it was one more thing that could never be acknowledged.)

The neighbor's wife herded us from the house. As we turned from the driveway onto the street, I looked back; firemen were carrying a stretcher down the one wide step from the front porch. The figure on it was draped with a brown blanket; even invisible, it had the same stiff, mysterious stillness it had had on the ironing board.

———

You can do things with your mind. You can speed things up, surround the suicide with words, contain the explosion, tidy up the kitchen. Your mind can repaint the walls and ceiling, install new, fireproof metal cabinets, and lay scorchproof linoleum on the floor. In the mind's kitchen, the squat, ancient refrigerator, with its cooling coils in a kind of turban on top, capable of generating a spark, perhaps, as they cycle on and off, is pasted over with a tall, cool, sleek rectangle. The electric oven, high up on the wall, can do no worse than scorch the meat. In this desperate kitchen my moth   an still move efficiently between her red tin recipe box and the ᴄ   ᴛ, baking her bread, her pies, her cakes, posing as the sanitized kitchen goddess, the star of our family mythology.

But the mind knows she was never really like that. She was the full Fury, the dark side of hell, as cold and calculating a witch as ever stirred a cauldron. All the mind's imaginings can't paste over her black act. Her suicide is seared into my brain; the burned kitchen with its body remains, an afterimage, flashing along the optic nerve no matter what other reality enters my eye.

———

The night before, she had sat in the wing chair in the living room, her eyes swimming with tears, staring straight ahead at nothing. Frightened, as always, by her remoteness and her desperation, I had walked hesitantly into the room and stopped. I brought good news; Hal, my middle brother, the oldest at home, had decreed that we children would stop fighting at the dinner table. We would do the dishes every night. It was important to tell my mother about this because a few minutes earlier, when our usual suppertime quarrels had begun (my father was working in New York, coming home only on weekends), she had stood up and announced to my youngest brother and I, the bitterest arguers, "If you two don't stop fighting, I'm going to kill myself."

And now she had. . . .

———

She had considered an alternative. My uncle once told me that she had gone to her mother-in-law, my grandmother, a small, patrician woman who sat on her Sheraton sofa with her straight back never touching the upholstery. My grandmother offered my mother coffee. After my mother said what was on her mind, my grandmother looked at her through her gold-framed pince-nez and said, "In this family, we do not divorce."

Between that meeting and her suicide, my mother spoke to a friend of hers, the mother of the girl my oldest brother later married. It was my sister-in-law who, years later, told me how my mother had driven her mother home one afternoon. When she pulled into the driveway, my mother leaned back, her hands still on the ˙ eel, and asked, "Do you ever feel that you just can't take it anymoi

This isn't much to go on. There have, of course, been family speculations: One of my brothers once said that he wondered whether our father had taken a mistress during the war, and our mother had found him out. My stepmother and my aunt believed my mother had a terrible secret that she was too noble to tell any of us: she was dying anyway, of cancer. Even I have wondered whether an early menopause contributed to a deep, unassuageable despair.

There is one fact: My uncle, my father's only brother, once told me that my mother chose to kill herself on the anniversary of the day she had promised to marry my father.

———

A suicide stops time. Before it happens, it is unimaginable. When it does happen, it feels unreal, out of time. Illness prepares you for death, and you can explain an accident. You can rail away at fate, or get angry at the other person, or even at the person who was killed, for being drunk at the wheel, or careless. You can be stunned, but you can grieve.

You can't get angry at a suicide, and you can't grieve. If you ask *why?* any possible answer seems to implicate you. Your questions become guilty: *How did I fail her? What could I have done?*

No one wants to deal with these questions. To avoid them, the family provides the suicide with conventionally dramatic occasions, like menopause or adultery or cancer. If my mother sacrificed herself to spare us the pain of her cancer, she was beyond human frailty— beyond our failures of sympathy, of empathy, of word, of act. If she was holy and perfect, we were off the hook, our guilt redeemed.

We were also sane, and so was she. A suicide is an extreme act. Without a motive, it seems a defeat of the self, a pointless punishment—incomprehensible, perhaps even mad. And the implications of madness are as disturbing as those of motive: *If she was mad, what were we? What are we now?*

What we are is this: Of her four children, one is manic-depressive; on lithium, the classic drug. The other three of us are, to varying degrees, chronically depressed. All of which could be the work of an inherited trait or disease. And that rai   the question whether depression as a mere set of malfunctionir eurons, with no relation to circumstance, could have driven my mother to kill herself.

I suppose that, in theory, it could have; a clinical depression can make the act of living feel too painful to go on with. But my mother's suicide clearly had great meaning for her; she chose its form and its time so carefully, carried it out so well. I think her depression became unbearable as her life became unbearable—because she no longer perceived any possibility of a future inside or outside of marriage. To stay alive is to project yourself into the future every second; to lose your future is a kind of death-in-life.

Today, of course, she would probably have gotten a divorce. But in 1949 or 1950 it wasn't easy for a middle-aged woman with four children to initiate divorce proceedings, especially if nobody in her family was backing her up. To prove cause, she would have had to charge my father with something like adultery, which he probably had never committed. It would have been very difficult for her to contemplate, much less go through, the messy, tawdry business of accusations, the establishment of proof.

She wouldn't have liked the image the world would pin on her after she slammed the door, either. She cared, almost desperately, for the proprieties, but divorced women were called *divorcées,* a term suggestive of wickedness and irresponsibility, with definite overtones of promiscuity.

Marriage was still how women made a living. As a single parent— almost unheard of in the middle classes at that time—what would she have done for money? She was probably too much of an idealist to plan on alimony, and even if she had thought of it she may, given my father's notorious stinginess, have despaired of the possibility of actually receiving it. She certainly would not have looked forward to continuing to be financially dependent on him. But she hadn't held a job in twenty years. There weren't any support groups to help her invent a résumé and role-play a job interview. "Life experience" had no currency in the marketplace. It must have seemed to her that if she dropped out, she'd be gone.

I don't think any of this is enough to explain why she chose death, though. They may all be factors, but next to th   he word *suicide* still sounds extreme, suggests something that take   ace not in what we like to think of as daily life but in another dimension, in which the chain of cause and effect has gone awry, so that apparently ordinary acts or situations lead to consequences that are tragic beyond bearing. The dimension in which Clytemnestra operated, and Medea. And my mother.

Who was, in her own way, a tragic heroine too, victim and villain both, like her great predecessors. Revenge was certainly on her mind; her suicide ruined my father's career. He never quite forgave her for that; it must have seemed like another strand in the web of a fate he set himself to deny at all costs.

High tragedy may seem improbable in an age of quantum mechanics, when things happen randomly all over the universe: Identify a photon, and the next second you have no idea where it is. Take a cruise, and you wind up being shot by terrorists and thrown overboard before your wife's eyes. Take a plane, and a bomb explodes under your seat, ejecting you without a parachute, to plummet into the sea next to an equally astonished infant.

But this suicide, like all real tragedies, was a family affair. The Greeks and Shakespeare understood what we deny; that, in families, actions almost always have a reason. Fate is tied to character, and even the gods are led by their vices, their desires, and their weaknesses.

In a family, lives are tangled together, so that parents confuse each other, their sons, and their daughters with their own pasts. The present can reverberate so strongly with the cries of the parents' former selves that a betrayed wife can come to see nothing but doom where an outsider sees something simple, rational, and finite—a decision to move to another place, say. An option. Nothing very extreme, certainly.

And all the while, the futures of the sons and daughters are created or canceled, depending on whether their parents allow them to escape or suck them into their games, so that the parents' despair endures as the children's painful, eternal present.

Although I don't think my mother meant to include me in her revenge, she and I were hopelessly intertwined by our gender and my youth, and by the peculiar ways in which I   ved her needs and, later, the family's. She had seen in me a mirror (erself, and so had always seemed to me to be my particular responsibility. To my brothers, who were boys and older, her suicide meant a shock, a loss, an interruption, feelings of guilt and anger to be denied; to me, it meant the end of any sense of myself as a separate person.

Of course, after all these years I realize intellectually that my mother's act may have had very little, perhaps nothing at all, to do with me. Yet I was, willy-nilly, deeply embroiled in her life, in secret aspects of her character that may have revealed themselves only in what happened between us. So each one in the family had a secret life with her, each child was shaped by her. And, being shaped, imagined being the shaper. . . .

———

I think that what was going on in my mother's head just before she killed herself was a continuation of the drama she had played out with me, when I was very small and she was driven to fury by my impulses and desires. Her rage then had been as much at herself as at me, because she saw me as part of herself. It was as if, in the face of my two-year-old needs, her fragile, hard-won sense of selfhood, of body-and-mind integrity, broke down, and she was overwhelmed by an avatar of her helpless infant self. In an act beyond empathy, denying all boundaries of age, of body, of size, of self, she *became* me, and I became her. She would make me perfect, because she couldn't endure imperfection in a piece of herself.

I was split by her madness. To survive, I took her path, on which, in conscious life, the good and the bad selves never meet. When she started out on that path, who had broken her? Was it her mother, that tiny, gentle survivor I knew? Someone must have set her on it. Yet she grew up, and married, and was thought to be an ordinary human being, a woman who had chosen her life, much like any other woman.

How can we know, in the wheel of the self, what we have chosen and what is forced upon us? And why, when so much else is possible, are we doomed to live with choices made in terror and desperation, at an age so young the selves we make can never fit the fabric of a later, larger life? . . .

———

My brothers and I all keep cats, because our mother was fond of cats and we grew up with them, as she did. Petting our cats gives us the feeling that physical affection is still a possibility. Those of us who have children didn't pet those children when they were small, any more than our mother petted us. The cats give it to us vicariously, as they did when she was alive.

As a child, I was consumed with the idea that there should be equal time for everybody. At night I would line up my dolls and stuffed animals so each one would get time next to my body. There was room for one on each side of me in bed; the rest lay on the floor in a row that extended, perpendicular to the plane of my body, from the bed out across the room.

Each night I would put the one that had been farthest out on the floor the night before onto the bed. For that night and the one following it would enjoy the bliss of sleeping next to my body, first on the wall side, then on the outer side. Then it would begin again its slow journey to the limbo of distance, staring straight up from the floor, unable even to see me. I, if I chose, might lean to see it, but sometimes I did not choose to. It pleased me to be remote.

When I think of my mother, she is always alone, too, even when I am with her. Her back is turned, or her head averted. Sometimes I still wish I could muscle in on her scene and force her to acknowledge me, because maybe then she would change her mind.

from

GIRL, INTERRUPTED

SUSANNA KAYSEN

1993

In her memoir Girl, Interrupted, *Susanna Kaysen enters the surreal world of a psychiatric ward where she spent time as a teenager in the 1960s. Diagnosed with borderline personality disorder, Kaysen looks at the madness that exists around her in a hospital, where such patients as Sylvia Plath, Robert Lowell, and Ray Charles also had been treated. Kaysen's account portrays the ward's various personalities, including her roommate whose emotional breakdown occurred in a movie theater and another patient who hoards chicken carcasses. A former freelance editor and proofreader, Kaysen published* Girl, Interrupted *almost thirty years after her hospitalization. In this selection, she describes the sensations of insanity.*

VELOCITY VS. VISCOSITY

Insanity comes in two basic varieties: slow and fast.

I'm not talking about onset or duration. I mean the quality of the insanity, the day-to-day business of being nuts.

There are a lot of names: depression, catatonia, mania, anxiety, agitation. They don't tell you much.

The predominant quality of the slow form   scosity.

Experience is thick. Perceptions are thickened and dulled. Time is slow, dripping slowly through the clogged filter of thickened perception. The body temperature is low. The pulse is sluggish. The immune system is half-asleep. The organism is torpid and brackish. Even the reflexes are diminished, as if the lower leg couldn't be bothered to jerk itself out of its stupor when the knee is tapped.

Viscosity occurs on a cellular level. And so does velocity.

In contrast to viscosity's cellular coma, velocity endows every platelet and muscle fiber with a mind of its own, a means of knowing and commenting on its own behavior. There is too much perception, and beyond the plethora of perceptions, a plethora of thoughts about the perceptions and about the fact of having perceptions. Digestion could kill you! What I mean is the unceasing awareness of the processes of digestion could exhaust you to death. And digestion is just an involuntary sideline to thinking, which is where the real trouble begins.

Take a thought—anything; it doesn't matter. I'm tired of sitting here in front of the nursing station: a perfectly reasonable thought. Here's what velocity does to it.

First, break down the sentence: *I'm tired*—well, are you really tired, exactly? Is that like sleepy? You have to check all your body parts for sleepiness, and while you're doing that, there's a bombardment of images of sleepiness, along these lines: head falling onto pillow, head hitting pillow, Wynken, Blynken, and Nod, Little Nemo rubbing sleep from his eyes, a sea monster. Uh-oh, a sea monster. If you're lucky, you can avoid the sea monster and stick with sleepiness. Back to the pillow, memories of having mumps at age five, sensation of swollen cheeks on pillows and pain on salivation—stop. Go back to sleepiness.

But the salivation notion is too alluring, and now there's an excursion into the mouth. You've been here before and it's bad. It's the tongue: Once you think of the tongue it becomes an intrusion. Why is the tongue so large? Why is it scratchy on the sides? Is that a vitamin deficiency? Could you remove the tongue? Wouldn't your mouth be less bothersome without it? There'd be more room in there. The tongue, now, every cell of the tongue, is ⟨ mous. It's a vast foreign object in your mouth.

Trying to diminish the size of your tongue, you focus your attention on its components: tip, smooth; back, bumpy; sides, scratchy, as noted earlier (vitamin deficiency); roots—trouble. There are roots to the tongue. You've seen them, and if you put your finger in your mouth you can feel them, but you can't feel them *with* the tongue. It's a paradox.

Paradox. The tortoise and the hare. Achilles and the what? The tortoise? The tendon? The tongue?

Back to tongue. While you weren't thinking of it, it got a little smaller. But thinking of it makes it big again. Why is it scratchy on the sides? Is that a vitamin deficiency? You've thought these thoughts already, but now these thoughts have been stuck onto your tongue. They adhere to the existence of your tongue.

All of that took less than a minute, and there's still the rest of the sentence to figure out. And all you wanted, really, was to decide whether or not to stand up.

Viscosity and velocity are opposites, yet they can look the same. Viscosity causes the stillness of disinclination; velocity causes the stillness of fascination. An observer can't tell if a person is silent and still because inner life has stalled or because inner life is transfixingly busy.

Something common to both is repetitive thought. Experiences seem prerecorded, stylized. Particular patterns of thought get attached to particular movements or activities, and before you know it, it's impossible to approach that movement or activity without dislodging an avalanche of prethought thoughts.

A lethargic avalanche of synthetic thought can take days to fall. Part of the mute paralysis of viscosity comes from knowing every detail of what's ahead and having to wait for its arrival. Here comes the I'm-no-good thought. That takes care of today. All day the insistent dripping of I'm no good. The next thought, the next day, is I'm the Angel of Death. This thought has a glittering expanse of panic behind it, which is unreachable. Viscosity flattens the effervescence of panic.

These thoughts have no meaning. They are idiot mantras that exist in a prearranged cycle: I'm no good, I'm the A   l of Death, I'm stupid, I can't do anything. Thinking the first tho ͜ t triggers the whole circuit. It's like the flu: first a sore throat, then, inevitably, a stuffy nose and a cough.

Once, these thoughts must have had a meaning. They must have meant what they said. But repetition has blunted them. They have become background music, a Muzak medley of self-hatred themes.

———

Which is worse, overload or underload? Luckily, I never had to choose. One or the other would assert itself, rush or dribble through me, and pass on.

Pass on to where? Back into my cells to lurk like a virus waiting for the next opportunity? Out into the ether of the world to wait for the circumstances that would provoke its reappearance? Endogenous or exogenous, nature or nurture—it's the great mystery of mental illness.

from

SEARCHING FOR MERCY STREET

LINDA GRAY SEXTON

1994

As the eldest daughter of the poet Anne Sexton, Linda Gray Sexton grew up in a household that was consumed by mental illness. Her mother's erratic behavior, psychoanalysis, hospitalizations, and eventual suicide defined Sexton's childhood and young adulthood in ways that she would not fully understand until writing her memoir Searching for Mercy Street *at the age of forty. As a novelist, Sexton has devoted much of her work to the complexities of family relationships.*

IN EXILE

My heart pounds and it's all I can hear—my
feeling for my children does not surpass my
desire to be free of their demands upon my
emotions. . . . What have I got? Who would want to
live feeling that way?

> —*February 6, 1957*
> *Anne Sexton to her psychiatrist,*
> *Dr. Martin Orne*

My story as a daughter and my mother's story   mother begins in a Boston suburb, back in the 1950s, when I was   led from my childhood home to make room for someone else: Mother's mental illness, which lived among us like a fifth person. At ages one and two and three, I could not understand that Anne Sexton's experiences with mental institutions, insanity, and the underside of her own unconscious would one day be put to good use in the crafting of a poetry recognized worldwide. I knew only that I was small and alone, sent off to live in the home of relatives until her "condition" improved; I had been taken away from my mother at the period of childhood in which separation anxiety is acute for even the most secure, beloved child. This rupture in the fabric of our family was the event that defined my childhood, just as her responsibility for casting me out was the event that defined her motherhood.

How I came to be exiled evolved into a legend with many variations, recounted by a number of narrators. My mother and my paternal grandmother, Nana, had each told me the story as I was growing up; while the details often differed, the basic theme, sung over and over, consisted of this: as a three-year-old I had overwhelmed my mother, my needs too intense for this fragile, dependent twenty-eight-year-old woman. Increasingly burdened, she was unable to care for me or my baby sister, Joy, and had had a psychotic break during which the voices in her head spoke so loudly she could hear nothing else.

> Ugly angels spoke to me. The blame,
> I heard them say, was mine. They tattled
> like green witches in my head, letting doom
> leak like a broken faucet;
> as if doom had flooded my belly and filled your bassinet,
> an old debt I must assume.

> —*"The Double Image"*

She had begun seeing a psychiatrist shortly following Joy's birth in August of 1955, when she began to feel disoriented, "unreal," and agitated. By March of 1956, this feeling had deepened, and she became terrified of being alone with Joy and me. At this point, whenever my father traveled for business, Mother found it impossible to eat, paced the house twirling her hair, or lay in her bed masturbating and crying. Her loss of control accelerated, and this manifested itself in alternating bouts of depression and rage—a rage wherein she often slapped me or tried to choke me. She saw faces on the wall and heard voices directing her to kill either herself or my sister and me. The delusion was strong enough that she wanted to tear the wallpaper off the wall from which the voices spoke, but she found herself frozen with fear.

In mid-July, to end her desperation, she decided to kill herself. She took down to the back porch the bottle of pills the doctor had prescribed to help her sleep. There she sat for a while, long enough for my father to discover her and call her psychiatrist, who hospitalized her for a three-week stay at Westwood Lodge, the same private mental clinic that had once treated her father for his alcoholism.

"I was too sick to be your mother," she elaborated as I grew old enough to listen to this story, her eyes mournful as she drew deeply upon the cigarette, a Salem menthol, that she held clasped in her long elegant fingers. With her black hair and eyes of aquamarine, she was as beautiful and dramatic a woman as a daughter could hope for. How I would pray to look just like her—tall, slender, statuesque, and dark.

Small and blond, with a shy smile and blue eyes that held a tentative expression, I had been, Mother said later, an impossible three-year-old. "You cried all the time," she explained. "You whined. You were a difficult, annoying child." She told the story of my childhood quite richly, as if it were a fairy tale about different people, people we didn't know and would never meet, people who had gone through a difficult time but who were living happily ever after now.

I averted my eyes with shame when she told me how hard I was to care for: perhaps my ugly nature was to blame for my mother's difficulties with being a mother. What I remembered from those early years was my own fear, the anxiety that lived inside me like a boa constrictor and made it hard to breathe. My mother had been hospitalized in a terrible place, my mother had left me, my mother—the center of my small universe—was as fragile and precarious as the translucent Limoges my Nana kept on high shelves at her house. Who knew when or how she would next break? The years would ᵒⁿᵍ suicide attempts, trances, fugue states, fits of rage—and depres   so intense that she sat for hours staring into space, or paced restlessly like an animal in a cage, or spoke to the voices inside her head. Fear was the four-letter word with which I lived, locked inside me like a dirty secret.

Before Mother's first hospitalization in the summer of 1956, when I turned three, Nana had always taken me to her home during the times Mother couldn't cope with me, and I had found it a place of warmth and love. After Joy's birth, however, Nana became physically debilitated herself, and caring for two small children was out of the question.

She came to pick up Joy, and Mother begged her not to, following her up the stairs to the bedroom. "Just give me another chance, Billie," she said. "I'm feeling better, I'll be all right now."

"You can't be serious, Anne," Nana answered. I was trailing behind the two women, and all of us now reached the landing.

"I *am* serious. I don't want you to take her!"

"Your doctor says Joy's to come with me. They're not safe with you." And with that, Nana, her jawline thrust forward, went in to pack up Joy's booties and blankets. Joy, the interloper in the bassinet, oblivious, the baby who brought no joy to me.

"But I'll be good—I won't hurt them even if Linda whines for an *hour!* I promise!"

My grandmother did not relent and when she had finished packing up, she set Joy in the crook of her arm and started down the stairs. "You can't take her!" Mother screamed, enraged.

Nana kept right on going, her shoulders square with determination.

Mother turned on me, eyes electric with hate. "It's all *your* fault," she shouted, putting her face down close to mine. "*Your* fault!" I sucked my thumb, cringing against the green-and-gold wallpaper. Mother turned and ran to her room, where she slammed the door. I could hear the sound of her cries through the wall.

Every child is engaged by a story in which she plays one of the main characters—even if cast as the villain rather than the heroine, even if the story recalls pain rather than happiness. Remembering such a story is also another way of validating the experience, a literal picking at the scab so a clean scar can form. For many years I retold the story in a detached manner, a classic ˒ of denying how much that moment at the head of the stairs hu ᴉe. It took time before I could acknowledge it with either anger or tears. A long time before I could acknowledge the fury and sadness that day created in me, or the hostility that choked me like a poisonous noose and made me resent Joy, whose birth had seemed the cause—however innocent—of my abandonment.

Though Nana had volunteered to take both of us again, my

mother's mother, Mary Gray, decided this would be too taxing for Nana. And so I was sent to the same lonely home in which Mother herself had been miserable as a child, cared for mostly by nursemaids and housekeepers; the same place the voices inside her mind had first made themselves heard; the same garden where the seeds of her mental instability had taken root. She remembered her own childhood as a time scarred with incidents of emotional pain. In their "big house with four garages," Mary and Ralph Harvey partied a lot, drank heavily, and expected their daughters to stay on the *qui vive,* an expression that meant they must be appropriately dressed and groomed and ready to receive visitors at any moment. Appearances took precedence, even at the dinner table, and any one of the three could be dismissed because her complexion rendered her unpresentable. Ralph used the strap to discipline his girls. These memories overflowed Mother's psychiatric sessions and later would fill her poetry.

My departure from my parents' house happened rapidly, a tumble down a long, rocky hill. Events moved too quickly for understanding; they packed me up and took me to Annisquam, a wealthy retirement and vacation community on the northern Massachusetts shore.

The Harveys were prosperous, Ralph having made a fine living running the woolen mill that bore his name, where my father also worked after he and my mother eloped in 1948. Daddy was a traveling salesman, assigned to the South and the Midwest, away from home a great deal. Once I arrived in Annisquam, my grandparents hired a young woman named Esther to care for me. My grandfather was a large, intimidating man with a deep voice and broad face. I have few memories of him, none of being touched, and I never knew his lap or his laugh. Each night, however, my grandmother Ga-ga did allow me to sit briefly on her lap in her rocking chair on the long porch that overlooked the ocean.

Mary Gray Harvey was a pretty, blond wor   , small of frame and a bit stout in her later years. Her clothes were impeccable, her jewelry elaborate. Her lap provided me comfort during this time of turmoil. The evening air felt cool against my flushed face as I, wrapped in a thick white towel, could come to her only fresh from my bath. Just past the strip of lawn, the rocky ledge plummeted to the lip of the sea, which glistened like a giant gray mirror streaked with fire, reflecting the sun as she lowered herself over the rim of the world, slowly, like a woman into her bath.

After dark each night, however, the voice of the wind and the surge of the ocean against the rocks frightened me. Wolves, I feared, skulked beneath my bed. I never got in or out of bed without leaping as far from the edge of the mattress as possible, feet up fast. Later Mother would take this memory of mine and use it in her poem "The Fortress."

> No,
> the wind's not off the ocean.
> Yes, it cried in your room like a wolf
> and your pony tail hurt you. That was a long time ago.

Within a month or two, fifty-five-year-old Ga-ga and Grampa also became frustrated and overwhelmed with housing a young child who suffered from nightmares and anxiety. And then, too, the amiable Esther, who had filled my lonely days with game after game, was scheduled to return to school as fall approached. Mother, however, was no better. I could not return home.

On the day before her twenty-eighth birthday, while my father was traveling in the Midwest, Mother attempted suicide with an overdose of Nembutal. Nana drove her to the Emergency Room to have her stomach pumped and then told my father over the telephone. Mother's psychiatrist, Dr. Martin Orne, hospitalized her at Glenside Hospital, a grim public institution totally unlike any other mental hospital to which she would ever be committed again. "Her family was not very sympathetic about her problems," commented Dr. Orne in 1990. "Seeing her at Glenside, they recognized that things were serious. Moreover, Glenside cost less than `¨¨` twood Lodge, and that mattered." Glenside was the hospital Motl ̣ ̣vrote about in her poem "You, Doctor Martin," the hospital where, she later described to me, she was strapped to a bed with her arms tied to prevent her from making any other attempts on her life.

> I speed through the antiseptic tunnel
> where the moving dead still talk

of pushing their bones against the thrust
of cure. And I am queen of this summer hotel
or the laughing bee on a stalk

of death. We stand in broken
lines and wait while they unlock
the door and count us at the frozen gates
of dinner. The shibboleth is spoken
and we move to gravy in our smock
of smiles. We chew in rows, our plates
scratch and whine like chalk

in school. There are no knives
for cutting your throat. I make
moccasins all morning.

While the Harveys neither understood nor empathized with their
daughter once she was an adult—any more than they had when she
was a child—they nevertheless did make an effort to help her through
the mental crisis she was undergoing by doing what they could to ease
her distress in a practical sense: they had taken me into their home,
they were paying some of Mother's psychiatric bills, and twice a week
they sent down their cleaning woman, Mary ("Me-me") La Crosse, so
that Anne would not be burdened by housework. Perhaps seeing their
daughter hospitalized at Glenside had sobered them just the way
Orne hoped it would.

Ga-ga sent me off to stay with my mother's sister Blanche, in Scit-
uate, Massachusetts, and once again I was condensed into a suitcase.
As they were growing up, Anne, Jane, and Blanche had rarely gotten
along, consumed as they were by jealousy, minute games of power,
and one-upmanship. Or, at least, so it seemed in the other's eyes. Intense
sibling rivalry flourished there like weeds in a neglected garden. Mary
and Ralph had been self-involved, distant parents, adults consumed
with their own problems; the three Harvey girls never stopped squab-
bling about whose turn it was, what belonged to whom, and who got
the most. Though we saw Jane and Blanche only at Christmastime,
and Ga-ga and Grampa equally rarely, my parents seemed to have no
compunction about leaving me with any of them.

"[My sisters] certainly didn't care about me—my awful sisters!" Mother confided to her psychiatrist, Dr. Orne, in 1961. "I still hate them." The fact that Blanche was willing to take me into her home did not appear on the scorecard of love my mother kept in her own mind.

How strange it seems that despite Blanche's ambivalent relationship with my mother, she did offer me the best foster care she could manage. As the middle sister, she had always played mediator within the family, the one who took care of the others; thus, she stepped forward at a time when Jane's situation was far more conducive to taking on a stray child. Jane lived close by, in Wellesley, in a large house. Her husband made a fine living and could have more easily provided for an extra child.

The Taylors, on the other hand, were poor. My uncle Ed, an alcoholic, had trouble keeping a job, and he hung around the house in an undershirt. Blanche already had two daughters, just in elementary school, as well as two sons, one my age and one Joy's age. She had no help with either her house or her children, and there were neither the emotional nor monetary means to care for—much less love—a fifth child who belonged to a sister about whom she felt, at best, ambivalent. In this place of exile, secrets fermented.

It was a long car ride to Aunt Blanche's, one made longer by fear. I was to sleep in my cousins Lisa and Mary's room and try to be brave. Soon my mother would be well and I would go back to Newton, they said. I tried not to wonder or to ask questions; I tried not to cry but failed.

I remember this: how desperately I wanted my doll, a floppy baby with a stuffed cloth body, her white-blond hair a match for my own. I needed a familiar object to confirm who I was, or, more important, a familiar body with which to cuddle. I would rock her in my arms like a good mother. Aunt Blanche telephoned to ask for her, and my parents promised to send her down. I checked the mailbox every day, but it rang empty as a drum. It hurt to be alone. It hurt to be forgotten.

I snuck into my cousin Harvey's room and stole his plastic ruler for a game I called "shoe man"; it got caught in a crack between the floorboards and snapped in half. My mistake with the ruler brought out Uncle Ed's strap. This strap was a snake that lived by eating the mistakes children made. The more you made, the bigger and stronger he got. I see my uncle now, how he moved toward me, slowly, a big sweaty man with a leather belt in his hand. We were in the master bedroom, and he wore only his undershirt and shorts. Sitting on the edge of the bed, he bent me across his lap, peeled my panties down, crushed my face against the white chenille bedspread. This was how he beat me. This was shame: stripped naked, butt under his rough palm, the fire of his snake on my skin.

No one rescued me, or any of my cousins: especially not at night, when we hid behind doors, under beds, in closets. The noise started downstairs, then spiraled upward, like the smell of something burning. Aunt Blanche's cries did not cover the sound of Uncle Ed's fist as he hit her. *Thud-thud, thud-thud,* a hammer striking a rubber mat. I counted the number of blows: if there were too few it would be worse for us. After a while there was silence. Then a click, the refrigerator door opening, the hum of its motor coming on. The sound of a bottle set down hard on the metal table. None of us children moved. We knew intermission when we heard it.

No one said *stop* as he lurched up the stairs. His voice wheedled our names, thick and sweet, as if he were tricking a dog to come over so he could whack it black and blue. No one stopped him. Did anyone care?

Even drunk, Uncle Ed was good at finding our hiding places.

My thumb, however, was an old friend. It had been with me as long as I could remember, and its comfort never left my side. It had a special taste: a little sweet, a little sweat. Thirty-seven years later I can still remember that taste and the way my thumb fit between the softness of my tongue and the hard roof of my palate. I might have gone to high school being a closet sucker if it hadn't been for Uncle Ed.

I remember this: me, three years old, hunkering down in front of a low bookcase that resides in that shadowy house of my memory. It stood beneath a window that let in a wash of ⁻ afternoon sunlight, and I squatted in front of it, running my finger: ˑr the fat books with their spines of bright colors. I wondered when I would be able to read them. Already being read to was my favorite activity—a way to escape. These were thick stories that would last long enough to provide a respite of many hours. My mouth watered as if they were food. Thumb in my mouth, I caressed the titles one at a time.

"Get that out of your mouth!"

Uncle Ed strode across the room and jerked me to my feet by one skinny arm. His face was close, right up against my cheek, the unshaven stubble prickly. His eyes held the same fury Mother's often had. I shrunk from the electricity there.

He rubbed the soggy, wrinkled skin of my thumb between his fingers, hard, and then squeezed until the nail turned white. It hurt, as if I had closed it in the car door. I held very still. Didn't speak. Didn't breathe. Already I knew the power of words: what they could make happen, what they could bring down on your head. I was learning fast.

"Next time," he whispered, "I'll cut that thumb off and scramble it in my eggs for breakfast."

With his angry eyes and ugly voice, he left no room for doubt, and so I lived with that threat, repeated often, whenever I forgot to get the thumb out of my mouth in time. Terrified, I tried to keep my hand mostly in my pocket. I did not understand why sucking my thumb was bad or why it made him so mad. Seeing me purse my lips around that tender little digit sent him sky-high—and that was all I needed to know.

These months away from my parents encompassed the most complete terror I have ever known. I wondered if perhaps my mother had died and I was never really going home. Perhaps I had killed her—me and my tears, my demands, my need to be loved. What had I done that I should be punished this way?

At night, I lay awake in the dark to plead my case with God. *If I am very good tomorrow could you please make my Mommy better? If I eat all the broccoli on my plate will you help me not to make a mistake? If I don't suck my thumb anymore maybe could I please go home?*

Nights, from my bed, I watched the moon shift its shape through the sky. After a while, I stopped praying, s   )ed talking to God after dark. At three I had learned the litany of   ;pair and knew its truth with all my being: depend on no one. Not the wide, empty sky, nor the distant yellow moon. Not a teacher, not a minister. Not God. Not grown-ups. No one will give you what you crave: a doll, a cuddle, permission to suck your lovely soggy thumb. No one will rescue you.

from

THE BEAST

TRACY THOMPSON

1995

On an overcast day in 1990, Tracy Thompson typed herself a brief note: "Right now I am thinking I want to die." After landing a new job as a journalist at The Washington Post, *she soon began to relive the despondency that had plagued much of her life. To save herself from the stranglehold of her mental illness, she checked herself into a local hospital, where she was placed under a twenty-four hour suicide watch. With a reporter's tenacity and curiosity, Thompson reports on the anatomy of depression in her memoir* The Beast. *In this excerpt, she chronicles the religious confusion that fed many of her childhood anxieties.*

It is deep in the night; morning is a mirage. And the thing I have dreaded has happened: the beast is outside my window. It is a mechanical beast, and it screams—steel against steel, a heavy thundering of weight. There is the oppressive sense of something huge and black. It is confined for now, but it threatens to bolt loose, breaking all natural laws; if I move, it might notice me. I lie motionless, trying not to breathe. The beast slows, grumbling, then shudders, slides, and finally comes to a raucous, banging stop outside my   dow. Somehow the silence is worse than the cacophony which pr   led it. It is a silence of something about to happen, broken at intervals by another metallic groan as the beast moves, muttering in its sleep. The fear is a bubble which rises from the pit of my stomach to my lips. Then there is a shadow in the doorway: my mother.

"It's a freight train, Tace," she says tiredly. "Go back to sleep." In a minute, I hear her voice across the hallway, in my parents' bedroom. "I swear, I think she can hear those trains the minute they leave the station in Chattanooga."

———

I am sitting on my mother's lap. She is kneeling or sitting cross-legged on a bare hardwood floor. I feel warm and happy. There is sunlight coming through the window in front of me, and a breeze moves the sheer curtains. I am laughing.

It is summer, and I am in the backyard, a shelter under a cool canopy of oak trees. My mother's chaise lounge rests on bare dirt, next to the duck pen. She is sitting with the mother of one of my playmates, and they are sipping iced tea from tall frosted metal glasses, and I should be comfortable. But I'm not. I feel a familiar, gnawing fear. What's wrong? Something's wrong. I keep waiting for it to happen. "It's so nice to sit back here when it's raining, the trees are so close you don't get wet at all," my mother is saying. Somehow that casual remark is branded in my brain as if she had said, "The Russians are bombing us," or, "I am dying." Those were the things I expected to hear.

———

Most of my early memories are like sunlight through a tree, dappled with dread. "My hill-and-dale girl," my mother called me. At night, after everybody was asleep, I would kneel at the cedar chest in my bedroom, making a shrine by spreading the white sheer curtains around me. There I would bargain with God for relief from this awful sense of guilt and impending disaster. If I could be good enough, my father would not lose his job, my mother would not die of cancer, our house would not burn down. I would go to bed holding a cross made of plastic that absorbed light and glowed for a while in the dark, hoping to drift to sleep while the emblem of my Savior watched over me, a magical purplish glow. But the glow oft   aded before sleep came. On some nights, I drifted in and out of an   :ious doze, snapped into consciousness by the crowing of my grandmother's rooster across the cornfield from my bedroom. It might be dawn; it might be three A.M. The sound, like the call of a mockingbird, years later, seemed an accusation aimed at me for sins I could not name.

Verily, I say unto thee, that this night, before the cock crows, thou shalt deny me thrice.

———

Anxiety was in the air, like a virus.

My mother was afraid. "I had a terrible dream last night," she said one day. The four of us were in the car, at the top of a hill deep in the countryside south of Atlanta. We had been "visiting," dropping by relatives' houses on a Sunday afternoon, an old Southern custom. Now it was late. Ahead of us, the sun had burned to a dull orange and was sinking behind a knotted bramble of bare tree branches, throwing shadows across monochrome fields marked with the stubble of last summer's corn. My mother was always having terrible dreams, prophecies of disaster or interminable slow-motion nightmares in which she could not escape the thing that was pursuing her. It was the legacy of her past: a childhood of poverty, the early loss of both parents, years of deprivation and abuse from relatives. From all of that she had salvaged her Southern fundamentalist faith. Jesus was her refuge, the one Being who had never deserted her or made her feel unworthy; she loved her Savior with the fervor of an abandoned child. But even kindly Jesus warned us of doomsday, and that was what she was talking about now. My sister and I leaned over the front seat; she sat beside my father as he drove, and looked into the sunset.

"The sun was blood-red, like it was the end of the world," she said.

"What happened in the dream, Mama?" Her words gave me a chill. "Were we in it?"

"Yes," she said, shortly. Then she shuddered. "I don't want to talk about it." No matter how I pressed her, she would not say more. I leaned back into the car seat. How horrible it must have been, that she couldn't tell us. The dream was an omen; I believed in omens. We expected the end of the world, the Second Coming of Christ. It could happen at any moment. *For no man knows the da   he hour. I will come on thee as a thief, and thou shalt not know what hour I w   me upon thee. The sun shall be darkened, and the moon shall not give her light, and the stars of heaven shall fall, and the powers that are in heaven shall be shaken.* But I knew what her dream was about: it was about me, being left behind. I was not going to heaven.

I could not remember a time when I did not know that. The faith that steeled my mother for life, which my father accepted and which seemed to come so naturally for my older sister, did not come naturally to me.

From the beginning, my confusion centered on this thing called the Second Coming. It was supposed to be the moment of ultimate rapture for all Christians, when believers were to be caught up in the air and taken directly to heaven. We heard the Bible verses in church. *I tell you, in that night there shall be two men in one bed; the one shall be taken and the other shall be left... Two men shall be in the field; the one shall be taken, and the other left.* It was a moment all Christians supposedly longed for. But every description sounded terrible, disorienting, and strange to me. I just didn't get it. And the fact that this alternate view made no sense, that I awaited the Second Coming with horror and dread, was proof of my difference from others. And different, to a child, was a curse. Different meant defective.

"I can't feel at home in this world anymore," we sang in church. But the world *was* my home. I was in love with the tangible; in my mind, even the letters of the alphabet possessed shape, color, texture, weight.

This was Georgia, twenty miles south of Atlanta. The time was the early sixties.

One night when I was seven, President Kennedy was on television. I said, "What is it?" The adults stared at the television and did not answer. Afterwards, we had a family conference around the round oak kitchen table about what to do if a nuclear bomb fell on Atlanta. Do not get on the bus, my mother ordered; I will come get you, no matter what. At church, pale men in dark horn-rimmed glasses bent over me and asked me to suppose that godless Russians had threatened to shoot me if I did not renounce Jesus Christ. What would I do? I would renounce Jesus and go home, I thought; maybe then they would leave me alone. But I didn't say that. Telling th   le men that I was ready to knuckle under to the godless Russians '   not what they wanted to hear.

The imminence of nuclear war, centered around someplace called Cuba, got tangled up in my mind with the Second Coming. I couldn't decide which scared me more: the godless Russians or Jesus in the sky, coming to judge the quick and the dead. Somehow I always thought both events would take place directly over the marquee of the Roosevelt Drive-In Theater, visible from our back doorstep.

My mother remembers one Fourth of July in either 1962 or 1963. She and my father had stepped out into the driveway around midnight to watch the annual fireworks show put on by the drive-in. My sister and I were asleep, they thought, in the back bedroom. At some point, between whistles and pops, she became aware of screaming from the back of the house. It was the two of us, awakened by the noise. We thought it was the end of the world.

I have no memory of this event. I knew only that annihilation loomed. It could happen while I was asleep, while I was pulling up my socks, while I was fighting with my sister; I could wake up from a nap and discover myself doomed to eternal hell while the rest of my family had gone to heaven in the Great Rapture or the giant mushroom cloud, whichever came first. . . .

———

There were clear signs on at least one side of my family—my father's—that a vulnerability to mood disorders was woven into the family genes.

At some point in the 1930s, one story went, my father's mother simply went to bed and stayed there for a decade. No one knew exactly why, though there was some vague mention of "female troubles." In retrospect, it seems she simply gave up on life. By the time I formed my first memories of my father's mother, she was a bent woman, frailer and more elderly than her years, who sat on the sofa and seemed to absorb all the light and levity in the room. Her need for human contact—any kind—was insatiable, but her usual way of asking for it was to request personal favors. "Would you trim my toenails?" she would ask. "Would you wash my hair?"

Years later, as an adult, I learned of another child—a girl born before my father, whose existence my grandmother rarely spoke of. Her name was Helen Faye. She had died at the age of three in a household accident. While my grandmother's back was turned, Helen Faye managed to climb up on a stool near the stove, where she upset a pot of boiling water. She died several days later. My father was sent to live with his aunt in Gadsden, Alabama, while his older brother stayed at home to help care for their mother.

My father's father was a roguishly handsome man who was one of Birmingham's first motorcycle policemen. No one in the family ever heard my grandmother call him anything but "Boy"—not in the demeaning sense also known then in the South, as addressed to black men, but as a simple word of endearment, an unusual gesture in a woman so reticent. At some point after Helen Faye's death, he left. In some versions of the story, he simply departed—went out for a pack of cigarettes, as the saying goes, and never came back; in other versions, they had fought over his decision to go look for work in Mobile. His brother found him, years later, working on the docks in San Francisco. When I was an infant, my mother says, there came news that he had remarried. My grandmother was living with my parents then— she spent most of her life, after her bedridden period, shuttling from one son's house to the other—and my mother was awakened in the night by the sound of racking sobs. By then, he had been gone for several years. My grandmother still wore her wedding ring.

So death and abandonment took up residence in our house, trapped under a blanket of suffocating silence, and for comfort there was a kindly Jesus who might come at any moment to judge the quick and the dead.

Of my mother's family I know even less. She has a picture, taken about 1929, of two little girls standing against the side of a house. It appears to be morning. Both have bobbed hair and are carrying Easter baskets. The older one, about seven, looks directly into the camera. The younger one, who is about three, is looking off to one side—distracted for the moment by a butterfly, perhaps, or the appearance of the family cat. Looming across the foreground of that picture are two large shadows, a man and a woman, evidently the adults who are taking the picture. The three-year-old is my mother. The shadows are her only visible reminder of her parents.

She never knew her father. He left not ng after that, for reasons never explained, the way men left families in the Depression to seek work elsewhere or simply to rid themselves of the burdens of a wife and children. My mother was told that he had died. She has only vague memories of her mother—a serious, deeply religious woman with auburn hair, who worked in the Nabisco factory in downtown Atlanta, making biscuit boxes. She died of influenza when my mother was four, the winter after that Easter snapshot was made. My aunt—the seven-year-old in that picture—was told that as their mother was dying, she made her own sister promise to take care of her two little girls.

The promise was casually made and just as casually broken; poverty had made my mother's family bitter and mean-spirited. Two children, to them, simply meant a bigger grocery bill. Neither my mother nor her sister has ever spoken of their relatives with anything approaching affection. The only uncle who was financially stable, an accountant with Coca-Cola, did petition to adopt them. But the courts refused to give him custody, citing his alcoholism. For a time, my mother and her sister shuttled between the homes of various relatives, treated like the unwanted children they were. My mother remembers a family argument that ended with the two of them being pushed out of a car and left by the side of a deserted road in the country. How long they were there she does not remember; it seemed like a week, though it was probably not more than an hour. She remembers standing there with her sister in the tall grass, watching the car drive away. She was six years old; her sister was ten.

The two of them wound up as full-time residents of the Southern Christian Children's Home in downtown Atlanta. During one particularly lean period, money was so scarce that the children got a piece of bread with some pasty peanut butter for dinner at night. My mother learned to eat the bread and save the peanut butter, rolling it into a ball to eat in bed at night before she went to sleep.

My aunt left the children's home at sixteen to make an unwise marriage. My mother was luckier: she was adopted at the age of eight. Not surprisingly, she lavished her unqualified adoration on the man who came to her rescue. He was a rawboned Georgia farmer named John Derrick, whose wife, Cora, could not have ch˙ ˙ ᴈn. I called him Pa-Pa. By the time I was four or five, he was retir   rom Southern Railway, the job he had taken to pay the bills. But at heart he was still a farmer, and up to the year before he died, he was still reflexively putting seeds in the soil. One of my earliest memories is of sitting on his lap while he fished a knife out of a front pocket of his worn overalls to peel an apple for me.

My memories of those years are primitive and sensory.

The dirt road out front is red clay, gluey and slick when wet. I dig it out from under my nails, find it between my toes. I walk behind my grandfather, Pa-Pa, as he plows the upper cornfield with his white mule, Becky. It is early spring, and the crumbling clots of dirt are cold, as if the plow is opening up the winter earth to the steady spring sun. The dirt smells dark, a musky scent of manure and rain.

Later, in another spring, I remember lying on the earth outside the barn, across a dirt lane from where Pa-Pa plowed. He died on a spring day like this, a day like an old lady's idea of heaven: a little too hot, a little too perfumed, a little too floral. I smell honeysuckle. Running under that scent, like the harsh one-note plaint of a diggery doo, is a faint animal stench from the barn. The sun is hot on my back. I lie facedown in the grass, my face pressed to the earth, and while I sleep it seems I can feel the earth move, almost imperceptibly, toward late afternoon.

from

"BLACK SWANS"

LAUREN SLATER

1996

Three years after graduating from college, Lauren Slater was diag-nosed with obsessive-compulsive disorder. Unable to concentrate and badgered by an inexplicable urge to count and repeat rituals, she visited a behavioral psychologist and was later prescribed the antidepressant Prozac. Slater's essay "Black Swans" searches for meaning in her mental illness and the course of her recovery. Now a psychologist her-self, she has written widely not only about her own madness but also about the troubled minds of her patients.

There is something satisfying and scary about making an angel, low-ering your bulky body into the drowning fluff, stray flakes landing on your face. I am seven or eight and the sky looms above me, grey and dead. I move my arms and legs—expanding, contracting—sculpting snow before it can swallow me up. I feel the cold filter into my head, seep through the wool of my mittens. I swish wider, faster, then roll out of my mould to inspect its form. There is the imprint of my head, my arms which have swelled into white wings. I step back, step for-ward, pause and peer. Am I dead or alive down there? Is this a picture of heaven or hell? I am worried about where I ⋯ go when I die, that each time I swallow an invisible stone will ge   ght in my throat. I worry that when I eat a plum, a tree will grow in my belly, its branches twining around my bones, choking. When I walk through a door I must tap the frame three times. Between each nighttime prayer to Yahweh I close my eyes and count to ten and a half.

And now I look down at myself sketched in the snow. A familiar anxiety chews at the edges of my heart, even while I notice the beauty of the white fur on all the trees, the reverent silence of this season. I register a mistake on my angel, what looks like a thumbprint on its left wing. I reach down to erase it, but unable to smooth the snow perfectly, I start again on another angel, lowering myself, swishing and sweeping, rolling over—no. Yet another mistake, this time the symmetry in the wingspan wrong. A compulsion comes over me. I do it again, and again. In my memory hours go by. My fingers inside my mittens get wrinkled and raw. My breath comes heavily and the snow begins to blue. A moon rises, a perfect crescent pearl whose precise shape I will never be able to recreate. I ache for something I cannot name. Someone calls me, a mother or a father. *Come in now, come in now.* Very early the next morning I awaken, look out my bedroom window, and see the yard covered with my frantic forms—hundreds of angels, none of them quite right. The forms twist and strain, the wings seeming to struggle up in the winter sun, as if each angel were longing for escape, for a free flight that might crack the crystal and ice of her still, stiff world.

Looking back on it now, I think maybe those moments in the snow were when my OCD began, although it didn't come to me full-fledged until my mid-twenties. OCD stands for obsessive-compulsive disorder, and some studies say over three million Americans suffer from it. The "it" is not the commonplace rituals that weave throughout so many of our lives—the woman who checks the stove a few times before she leaves for work, or the man who combs his bangs back, and then again, seeking symmetry. Obsessive-compulsive disorder is pervasive and extreme, inundating the person's life to the point where normal functioning becomes difficult, maybe even impossible.

For a long time my life was difficult but not impossible. Both in my childhood and my adulthood I'd suffered from various psychiatric ailments—depressions especially—but none of these were as surreal and absurd as the obsessive-compulsive disorder that one day presented itself. Until I was twenty-five or so, I don't think I could have been really diagnosed with OCD, although my memory of the angels indicates I had tendencies in that direction. I was a child at once nervous and bold, a child who loved trees that trickled sap, the Vermont fields where grass grew the color of deep-throated rust. I was a child who gathered earthworms, the surprising pulse of pink on my fingers, and yet these same fingers, later in the evening, came to prayer points, searching for safety in the folds of my sheets, in the quick counting rituals.

Some mental health professionals claim that the onset of obsession is a response to an underlying fear, a recent trauma, say, or a loss. I don't believe that is always true because, no matter how hard I think about it, I remember nothing unusual or disorienting before my first attack, three years out of college. I don't know exactly why at two o'clock one Saturday afternoon what felt like a seizure shook me. I recall lying in my apartment in Cambridge. The floors were painted blue, the curtains a sleepy white. They bellied in and out with the breezes. I was immersed in a book, *The Seven Story Mountain,* walking my way through the tale's church, dabbing holy water on my forehead. A priest was crooning. A monk moaned. And suddenly this: A thought careening across my cortex. I CAN'T CONCENTRATE. Of course the thought disturbed my concentration, and the monk's moan turned into a whisper, disappeared.

I blinked, looked up. I was back in Cambridge on a blue floor. The blue floor suddenly frightened me; between the planks I could see lines of dark dirt, and the sway of a spider crawling. Let me get back, I thought, into the world of the book. I lowered my eyes to the page, but instead of being able to see the print, there was the thought blocking out all else: I CAN'T CONCENTRATE.

Now I started to panic. Each time I tried to get back to the book the words crumbled, lost their sensible shapes. I said to myself *I must not allow that thought about concentration to come into my mind anymore,* but, of course, the more I tried to suppress it, the louder it jangled. I looked at my hand. I ached for its familiar skin, the pale   of its palm and the three threaded lines that had been with me sin   irth, but as I held it out before my eyes, the phrase I CAN'T CONCENTRATE ON MY HAND blocked out my hand, so all I saw was a blur of flesh giving way to the bones beneath, and inside the bones the grimy marrow, and in the grimy marrow the individual cells, all disconnected. Shattered skin.

My throat closed up with terror. For surely if I'd lost the book, lost language, lost flesh, I was well on my way to losing the rest of the world. And all because of a tiny phrase that forced me into a searing self-consciousness, that plucked me from the moment into the meta-moment so I was doomed to think about thinking instead of thinking other thoughts. My mind devouring my mind.

I tried to force my brain onto other topics but with each mental dodge I became aware that I was dodging, and each time I itched I became aware that I was itching, and with each inhalation I became aware that I was inhaling, and I thought *if I think too much about breathing, will I forget how to breathe?*

I ran into the bathroom. There was a strange pounding in my head, and then a sensation I can only describe as a hiccup of the brain. My brain seemed to be seizing as the phrase about concentration jerked across it. I delved into the medicine cabinet, found a bottle of aspirin, took three, stood by the sink for five minutes. No go. Delved again, pulled out another bottle—Ativan, a Valium-like medication belonging to my housemate Adam. Another five minutes, my brain still squirting. One more Ativan, a tiny white triangle that would put me to sleep. I would sleep this strange spell off, wake up me again, sane again. I went back to my bed. The day darkened. The Ativan spread through my system. Lights in a neighboring window seemed lonely and sweet. I saw the shadow of a bird in a tree, and it had angel wings, and it soared me someplace else, its call a pure cry.

"What's wrong with you?" he said, shaking my shoulder. My housemate Adam stood over me, his face a blur. Through cracked eyelids I saw a wavering world, none of its outlines resolved: the latticed shadow of a tree on a white wall, my friend's face a streak of pink. I am O.K., I thought, for this was what waking up was always like, the gentle resurfacing. I sat up, looked around.

"You've been sleeping for hours and   rs," he said. "You slept from yesterday afternoon until now."

I reached up, gently touched a temple. I felt the far-away nip of my pulse. My pulse was there. I was here.

"Weird day yesterday," I said. I spoke slowly, listening to my words, testing them on my tongue. So far so good.

I stood up. "You look weird," he said, "unsteady."

"I'm O.K.," I said, and then, in that instant, a surge of anxiety. I had lied. I had not been O.K. *Say God I'm sorry fourteen times* I ordered myself. *This is crazy* I said to myself. *Fifteen times* a voice from somewhere else seemed to command. "You really all right?" Adam asked. I closed my eyes, counted, blinked back open.

"O.K.," I said. "I'm going to shower."

———

But it wasn't O.K. As soon as I was awake, obsessive thoughts returned. What before had been inconsequential behaviors like counting to three before I went through a doorway or checking the stove several times before bed, now became imperatives. There were a thousand and one of them to follow: rules about how to step, what it meant to touch my mouth, a hot consuming urge to fix the crooked angles of the universe. It was constant, a cruel nattering. *There, that tilted picture on the wall. Scratch your head with your left hand only.* It was noise, the beak of a woodpecker in the soft bark of my brain. But the worst, by far, were the dread thoughts about concentrating. I picked up a book but couldn't read, so aware was I of myself reading, and the fear of that awareness, for it meant a cold disconnection from this world.

I began to avoid written language because of the anxiety associated with words. I stopped reading. Every sentence I wrote came out only half coherent. I became afraid of pens and paper, the red felt tip bleeding into white, a wound. What was it? What was I? I could not recognize myself spending hours counting, checking, avoiding. . . .

I spent the next several weeks mostly in my bedroom, door closed, shades drawn. I didn't want to go out because any movement might set off a cycle of obsessions. I sat hunched and lost weight. My friend Adam, who had some anxiety problems of his own and was a real pooh-pooher of "talk therapy," found me a be   orist.

"These sorts of conditions," the behaviora   ychologist, Dr. Lipman, told me as I sat one day in his office, "are associated with people who have depressive temperaments, but, unlike depression, they do not yield particularly well to more traditional modes of psychotherapy. We have, however, had some real success with cognitive/behavioral treatments."

Outside it was a shining summer day. His office was dim though, his blinds adjusted so only tiny gold chinks of light sprinkled through, illuminating him in patches. He was older, maybe fifty, and pudgy, and had tufts of hair in all the wrong places, in the whorls of his ears and his nostrils. I had a bad feeling about him.

Nevertheless, he was all I had right now. "What is this sort of condition exactly?" I asked. My voice, whenever I spoke these days, seemed slowed, stuck, words caught in my throat. I had to keep touching my throat, four times, five times, six times, or I would be punished by losing the power of speech all together.

"Obsessive-compulsive disorder," he announced. "Only you," he said, and lifted his chin a little proudly, "have an especially difficult case of it."

This, of course, was not what I wanted to hear. "What's so especially difficult about my case?" I asked.

He tapped his chin with the eraser end of his pencil. He sat back in his leather seat. When the wind outside blew, the gold chinks scattered across his face and desk. Suddenly, the world cleared a bit. The papers on his desk seemed animated, rustling, sheaves full of wings, books full of birds. I felt creepy, despondent, and excited all at once. Maybe he could help me. Maybe he had some special knowledge.

He then went on to explain to me how most people with obsessive thoughts—*my hands are filthy*—for instance, always follow those thoughts with a compulsive behavior, like handwashing. And while I did have some compulsive behaviors, Dr. Lipman explained, I also reported that my most distressing obsession had to do with concentration, and that the concentration obsession had no clear-cut compulsion following in its wake.

"Therefore," he said. His eyes sparkled as he spoke. He seemed excited by my case. He seemed so sure of himself that for a moment I was back with language again, only this time it was his language, his words forming me.

"Therefore you are what we call a primary ruminator!"

A cow, I thought, chewing and chewing on the floppy scum of its cud. I lowered my head.

He went on to tell me about treatment obstacles. Supposedly "primary ruminators" are especially challenging because, while you can train people to cease compulsive behaviors, you can't train them nearly as easily to tether their thoughts. His method, he told me, would be to use a certain instrument to desensitize me to the obsessive thought, to teach me not to be afraid of it so, when it entered my mind, I wouldn't panic and thereby set off a whole cycle of anxiety and its partner, avoidance.

"How will we do it?" I asked.

And that is when he pulled "the instrument" from his desk drawer, a Walkman with a tiny tape in it. He told me he'd used it with people who were similar to me. He told me I was to record my voice saying "I can't concentrate I can't concentrate" and then wear the Walkman playing my own voice back to me for at least two hours a day. Soon, he said, I'd become so used to the thought it would no longer bother me.

He looked over at the clock. About half the session had gone by. "We still have twenty more minutes," he said, pressing the red recorder button, holding the miniature microphone up to my mouth. "Why don't you start speaking now."

I paid Dr. Lipman for the session, borrowed the Walkman and the tape, and then left, stepping into the summer light. . . . I did very little for the next year. Dr. Lipman kept insisting I wear the Walkman, turning up the volume, keeping it on for three, now four hours at a time. Fear and grief prevented me from eating much. When I was too terrified to get out of bed, Dr. Lipman checked me into the local hospital, where I lay amidst IV drips, bags of blood, murmuring heart machines that let me know someone somewhere near was still alive.

It was in the hospital that I was first introduced to psychiatric medications, which the doctors tried me on to no avail. The medications had poetic names and frequently rhymed with one another—Nortriptyline, Desipramine, Amitriptyline. Nurse ought me capsules in miniature paper cups, or oblong shapes of w   that left a salty tingle on my tongue. None of them worked, except to make me drowsy and dull.

And then one day Dr. Lipman said to me, "there's a new medication called Prozac, still in its trial period, but it's seventy-percent effective with OCD. I want to send you to a doctor here. He's one of the physicians doing trial runs."

I shrugged, willing to try. I'd tried so much, surely this couldn't hurt. I didn't expect much though. I certainly didn't expect what I finally got. . . .

On the first day of Prozac I felt nothing, on the second and third nausea, and then for the rest of that week headaches so intense I wanted to groan and lower my face into a bowl of crushed ice. I had never had migraines before. In their own way they are beautiful, all pulsing suns and squeezing colors. When I closed my eyes, pink shapes flapped and angels' halos spun. I was a girl again, lying in the snow. Slowly, one by one, the frozen forms lifted toward the light.

And then there really was an angel over me, pressing a cool cloth to my forehead. He held two snowy tablets out to me, and in a haze of pain I took them.

"You'll be all right," Adam said to me. When I cried it was a creek coming from my eyes.

I rubbed my eyes. The headache ebbed.

"How are you?" he asked.

"O.K.," I said. And waited for a command. *Touch your nose, blink twelve times, try not to think about think about concentrating.*

The imperatives came—I could hear them—but from far far away, like birds beyond a mountain, a sound nearly silent and easy to ignore.

"I'm . . . O.K.," I repeated. I went out into the kitchen. The clock on the stove ticked. I pressed my ear against it and heard, this time, a steady, almost soothing pulse.

Most things, I think, diminish over time, rock and mountain, glacier and bone. But this wasn't the nature of Prozac, or me on Prozac. One day I was ill, cramped up with fears, and the next day the ghosts were gone. Imagine having for years a raging fever, and then one day someone hands you a new kind of pill, and within a matter of hours sweat dries, the scarlet swellings go down, ur eyes no longer burn. The grass appears green again, the sky a g   e blue. *Hello hello. Remember me?* the planet whispers.

But to say I returned to the world is even a bit misleading, for all my life the world has seemed off-kilter. On Prozac, not only did the acute obsessions dissolve; so too did the blander depression that had been with me since my earliest memories. A sense of immense calm flooded me. Colors came out, yellow leaping from the light where it had long lain trapped, greens unwinding from the grass, dusk letting loose its lavender.

By the fourth day I still felt so shockingly fine that I called the Prozac Doctor. I pictured him in his office, high in the eaves of the hospital. I believed he had saved me. He loomed large.

"I'm well," I told him.

"Not yet. It takes at least a month to build up a therapeutic blood level."

"No," I said. "It doesn't." I felt a rushing joy. "The medicine you gave me has made me well. I've, I've actually never felt better."

A pause on the line. "I suppose it could be possible."

"Yes," I said. "It's happened." . . .

Every noon I took my pill. Instead of just placing it on my tongue and swallowing with water, I unscrewed the capsule. White powder poured into my hands. I tossed the plastic husk away, cradled the healing talc. I tasted it, a burst of bitterness, a gagging. I took it that way every day, the silky slide of Prozac powder, the harshness in my mouth.

Mornings now, I got up early to jog, showered efficiently, then strode off to the library. . . . I read with an appetite, hungry from all the time I'd lost to illness. The pages of the book seemed very white; the words were easy, black beads shining, ebony in my quieted mind. . . .

I could, I thought, do anything in this state of mind. I put my misgivings aside (how fast they would soon come back; how hard they would hit) and ate into my days, a long banquet. I did things I'd never done before, swimming at dawn in Walden Pond, writing poetry I knew was bad, and loving it anyway.

I applied for and was awarded a three-month grant to go to Appalachia, where I wanted to collect oral histories of mountain women. I could swagger anywhere on The Zack, on ¯¯ min P. Never mind that even before I'd ever come down with OC d been the anxious, tentative sort. Never mind that unnamed trepidations, for all of my life, had prevented me from taking a trip to New Hampshire for more than a few days. Now that I'd taken the cure, I really could go anywhere, even off to the rippling blue mountains of poverty, far from a phone or a friend.

———

A gun hung over the door. In the oven I saw a roasted bird covered with flies. In the bathroom, a fat girl stooped over herself without bothering to shut the door, and pulled a red rag from between her legs.

Her name was Kim, her sister's name was Bridget, and their mother and father were Kat and Lonny. All the females were huge and doughy while Lonny stood, a single strand of muscle tanned to the color of tobacco. He said very little while the mother and daughters chattered on, offering me Cokes and Cheerios, showing me to my room where I sat on a lumpy mattress and stared at the white walls.

And then a moon rose. A storm of hurricane force ploughed through fields and sky. I didn't feel myself here. The sound of the storm, battering just above my head, seemed far, far away. There was a whispering in my mind, a noise like silk being split. Next to me, on the night table, my sturdy bottle of Prozac. I was fine. So long as I had that, I would be fine.

I pretended I was fine for the next couple of days, racing around with manic intensity. I sat heavy Kat in one of her oversized chairs and insisted she tell me everything about her life in the Blue Ridge Mountains, scribbling madly as she talked. *I am happy happy happy* I sang to myself. I tried to ignore the strange sounds building in my brain, kindling that crackles, a flame getting hot.

And then I was taking a break out in the sandy yard. It was near one hundred degrees. The sun was tiny in a bleary sky. Chickens screamed and pecked.

In one swift and seamless move, Lonny reached down to grab a bird. His fist closed in on its throat while all the crows cawed and the beasts in my bones brayed away. He laid the chicken down on a stump, raised an ax, and cut. The body did its da   I watched the severing, how swiftly connections melt, how deep   d black is space. Blood spilled.

I ran inside. I was far from a phone or a friend. Maybe I was reminded of some pre-verbal terror: the surgeon's knife, the violet umbilical cord. Or maybe the mountain altitudes had thrown my chemistry off. I don't really know why, or how. But as though I'd never swallowed a Prozac pill, my mind seized and clamped and the obsessions were back.

I took a step forward and then said to myself *don't take another step until you count to twenty-five.* After I'd satisfied that imperative, I had to count to twenty-five again, and then halve twenty-five, and then quarter it, before I felt safe enough to walk out the door. By the end of the day, each step took over ten minutes to complete. I stopped taking steps. I sat on my bed.

"What's wrong with you?" Kat said. "Come out here and talk with us."

I tried, but I got stuck in the doorway. There was a point above the doorway I just had to see, and then see again, and inside of me something screamed *back again back again* and the grief was very large.

For I had experienced the world free and taken in colors and tasted grilled fish and moon. I had left one illness like a too tight snakeskin, and here I was, thrust back. What's worse than illness is to think you're cured—partake of cure in almost complete belief—and then with no warning to be dashed on a dock, moored.

Here's what they don't tell you about Prozac. The drug, for many obsessives who take it, is known to have wonderfully powerful effects in the first few months when it's new to the body. When I called the Prozac Doctor from Kentucky that evening, he explained to me how the drug, when used to treat OCD as opposed to depression, "peaks" at about six months, and then loses some of its oomph. "Someday we'll develop a more robust pill," he said. "In the meantime, up your dose."

I upped my dose. No relief. Why not? Please. Over the months I had come to need Prozac in a complicated way, had come to see it as my savior, half hating it, half loving it. I unscrewed the capsules and poured their contents over my fingers. Healing talc, gone. Dead sand. I fingered the empty husks.

"You'll feel better if you come to church v   us," Kat said to me that Sunday morning. She peered into my face, which must have been white and drawn. "Are you suffering from some city sickness?"

I shrugged. My eyes hurt from crying. I couldn't read or write; I could only add, subtract, divide, divide again.

"Come to church," Kat said. "We can ask the preacher to pray for you."

But I didn't believe in prayers where my illness was concerned. I had come to think, through my reading and the words of doctors, and especially through my brain's rapid response to a drug, that whatever was wrong with me had a simplistic chemical cause. Such a belief can be devastating to sick people, for on top of their illness they must struggle with the sense that illness lacks any creative possibilities.

I think these beliefs, so common in today's high-tech biomedical era where the focus is relentlessly reductionistic, rob illness of its potential dignity. Illness can be dignified; we can conceive of pain as a kind of complex answer from an elegant system, an arrow pointing inward, a message from soil or sky.

Not so for me. I wouldn't go to church or temple. I wouldn't talk or ask or wonder, for these are distinctly human activities and I'd come to view myself as less than human.

An anger rose up in me then, a rage. I woke late one night, hands fisted. It took me an hour to get out of bed, so many numbers I had to do, but I was determined.

And then I was walking, outside, pushing past the need to count before every step. The night air was muggy, and insects raised a chorus.

I passed midnight fields, a single shack with lighted windows. Cows slept in a pasture.

I rounded the pasture, walked up a hill. And then, before me, spreading out in moonglow, a lake. I stood by its lip. My mind was buzzing and jerking. I don't know at what point the swans appeared— white swans, they must have been, but in silhouette they looked black—that seemed to materialize straight out of the slumbering water. They rose to the surface of the water as memories rise to the surface of consciousness. Hundreds of black swans suddenly, floating absolutely silent, and as I stood there the counting ceased, my mind became silent, and I watched. The swans circled until it seemed, for a few moments, that they were inside of me, seven dark, silent birds, fourteen princesses, a single self swimming in a tepid sea.

I don't know how long I stood there, or when, exactly, I left. The swans disappeared eventually. The counting ticking talking of my mind resumed.

Still, even in chattering illness, I had been quieted for a bit; doors in me had opened; elegance had entered.

This thought calmed me. I was not completely claimed by illness, nor a prisoner of Prozac, entirely dependent on the medication to function. Part of me was still free, a private space not absolutely permeated by pain. A space I could learn to cultivate.

Over the next few days, I noticed that even in the thicket of obsessions my mind sometimes swam into the world, if only for brief forays. There, while I struggled to take a step, was the sun on a green plate. *Remember that* I said to myself. And here, while I stood fixated in a doorway, was a beetle with a purplish shell like eggplants growing in wet soil. *Appreciate this* I told myself, and I can say I did, those slivers of seconds when I returned to the world. I loved the beetle, ached for the eggplant, paddled in a lake with black swans.

And so a part of me began to learn about living outside the disease, cultivating appreciation for a few free moments. It was nothing I would have wished for myself, nothing to noisily celebrate. But it was something, and I could choose it, even while mourning the paralyzed parts of me, the pill that had failed me. . . .

Even after I raised my dose, the Prozac never worked as well as it once had, and years later I am sometimes sad about that, other times strangely relieved, even though my brain is hounded. I must check my keys, the stove; I must pause many times while I write this and do a ritual count to thirty. It's distracting, to say the least, but still I write this. I can walk and talk and play. I've come to live my life in those brief stretches of silence that arrive throughout the day, working at what I know is an admirable speed, accomplishing all I can in clear pauses, knowing those pauses may be short-lived. I am learning something about the single moment, how rife with potential it is, how truly loud its tick.

from

WILLOW WEEP FOR ME

MERI NANA-AMA DANQUAH

1998

At the age of nineteen, Meri Nana-Ama Danquah moved from Washington, D.C., to Los Angeles to pursue a career as a writer and performance artist. Her aspirations soon collapsed, however, as Danquah, a native of Ghana, withdrew into a state of bewildered helplessness. Isolated and disabled by grief and fatigue, she soon stopped showing up for her temp jobs and began slipping into a well of overwhelming sadness that she later identified as clinical depression. Willow Weep for Me, *one of the few books about black women and depression, traces Danquah's bouts with mental illness as she becomes a single mother and establishes herself as a journalist, poet, and teacher. The memoir is named for one of the author's favorite songs, "Willow Weep for Me," as performed by Billie Holiday.*

There are always fresh flowers and plants in my house. When they begin to die it is a sure sign that I, too, am beginning to wither. The window shades are never closed. Sunshine must always be visible. The bedroom is littered with no less than four alarm clocks. None display the same time. Some are as little as fifteen minutes ahead, others as much as one hour. Each night I set the c   s for a wake-up time of 6:00 AM. Rarely am I out of bed before 7:3   . Mornings have always been difficult.

For most of my life I have nurtured a consistent, low-grade melancholy; I have been addicted to despair. Because of my habitual tardiness, an eighth-grade teacher once scrawled these words of advice in my yearbook: *Once you learn to wake up in the morning, life will be a breeze.*

Though I have attended college in many places and at many times, I do not yet hold a degree. I have worked as a word processor, secretary, file clerk, waitress, arts administrator, phone sex operator, and creative writing instructor. I am often working-class broke. I am also a single mother. Life, for me, has hardly been "a breeze."

The majority of my days begin like this:

Barely awake, I head for the bathroom, stare into the mirror until I can identify the person staring back. There are still those mornings when my image seems foreign to me, when I move through my house like an intruder, fumbling over furniture and walking into walls, trying to avoid the temptation to crouch inside a corner and just zone out. "It gets better." I promise myself as I make my way into the living room, "This day *will* get better. It has to."

Having sworn off most chemical mood-altering substances, I choose music over coffee and cigarettes. Music eases my depressed mood. . . . Music and motion are the two things that can immediately touch the hurt inside of me. I can't begin to count the number of times I have circled Los Angeles in my car, traveling from one freeway onto the next without any particular destination, the tape player blasting tunes, my mouth open wide enough to scream lyrics.

There was a time when at any given moment I would abandon my bed, my lover, my apartment, to literally drive away the depression. The slow, gentle rhythm of automobiles, trains, and buses surrounds and soothes me, like an infant that is being cradled into calmness. But being a mother has changed the ways in which I mother myself. No matter how deep the despair or urgent the need to flee, I can't abandon my daughter. Nor can I drape her sleeping body in thick blankets, toss her over my shoulder like some runaway's sack and take her with me. She relies on my presence, my ability to cope.

Emotionally and physically taxing, the responsibilities of parenting are overwhelming for even the most stable person. Imagine them for someone with a history of depression stretching as far as a late-afternoon shadow. The daily tasks—bathing, ironing clothes, dressing, braiding hair, making breakfast, preparing lunch, school drop-offs and pick-ups—require every bit of what little get-up-and-go I have. However, they define my day. These responsibilities help me move past the temptation to rationalize myself right back into bed. Most times.

Afternoons and early evenings are usually my best and most productive times, when I am able to concentrate and focus without fatigue or anxiety. Sleep plays a major role in my efforts to maintain a balanced mood. I have found that too much is as disruptive as not enough. Late evenings, like mornings, take a harsh toll. I vacillate from insomnia to hypersomnia, from not being able to get a wink of rest to oversleeping and constantly feeling drugged with exhaustion.

We have all, to some degree, experienced days of depression. Days when nothing is going our way, when even the most trivial events can trigger tears, when all we want to do is crawl into a hole and ask "Why me?" For most people, these are isolated occurrences. When the day ends, so too does the sadness. But for some, such as myself, the depression doesn't lift at the end of the day or disappear when others try to cheer us up. These feelings of helplessness and desperation worsen and grow into a full-blown clinical depression. And when depression reaches clinical proportions, it *is* truly an illness, not a character flaw or an insignificant bout with the blues that an individual can "snap out of" at will.

———

Our reality often comes to us in fragments. From 1989 to 1994, I experienced several episodes of major depression. I prolonged the pain with silence, mostly because I was afraid—of being misunderstood or ostracized, of losing friends, of losing respect. Unless it has touched your life, depression can be a difficult disease to understand. I certainly would have never thought to consider myself a depressive. Clinical depression simply did not exist within the realm of my possibilities; or, for that matter, within the realm of possibilities for any of the black women in my world.

The illusion of strength has been and c   nues to be of major significance to me as a black woman. The one myth that I have had to endure my entire life is that of my supposed birthright to strength. Black women are *supposed* to be strong—caretakers, nurturers, healers of other people—any of the twelve dozen variations of Mammy. Emotional hardship is *supposed* to be built into the structure of our lives. It

went along with the territory of being both black and female in a society that completely undervalues the lives of black people and re-
gards all women as second-class citizens. It seemed that suffering, for
a black woman, was part of the package.

Or so I thought. . . .

You've heard descriptions of depression before: A black hole; an
enveloping darkness; a dismal existence through which no light
shines; the black dog; darkness, and more darkness. But what does
darkness mean to me, a woman who has spent her life surrounded by
it? The darkness of my skin; the darkness of my friends and family. I
have never been afraid of the dark. It poses no harm to me. What is the
color of my depression?

Depression offers layers, textures, noises. At times depression is as
flimsy as a feather, barely penetrating the surface of my life, hovering
like a slight halo of pessimism. Other times it comes on gradually like
a common cold or a storm, each day presenting new signals and symptoms until finally I am drowning in it. Most times, in its most superficial and seductive sense, it is rich and enticing. A field of velvet
waiting to embrace me. It is loud and dizzying, inviting the tenors and
screeching sopranos of thoughts, unrelenting sadness, and the sense of
impending doom. Depression is all of these things to me—but darkness, it is not. . . .

Medical science has no cure for depression. Therapy and antidepressants are merely treatments. Despite current advancements in the
treatment of depressive disorders, doctors still know very little about
them. The supposed facts and statistics that are disseminated about
depressive disorders are discouraging: the ratio of women to men that
are diagnosed with depression is 2 to 1; over half of the people who
have survived depression will most likely find themselves battling it
again sometime down the line; depression is   re common among
first-degree blood relatives of people with the   order.

Add to all this the social and economic realities of women, blacks,
single parents, or any combination of the three, and my chances for a
life that is free of depression appear to be slim. I, and others like me,
seem to be doomed right from the get-go. While I recognize the importance of such information, I regard most of the data as blather and
refuse to embrace it.

Personally, I choose to believe that somewhere, somehow, there is a cure for depression. I have to. But I think the healing, the reversal, must take place in the spirit, as well as the body. Therapy is crucial. Often I am asked whether the depressions I have are emotional or bio-chemical. Having posed that question myself a million times before, I am well aware of its implications, that an emotional depression is less profound, more topical because it is issue-related, and has very little to do with one's brain chemistry. As all our emotions and moods are biochemically induced, regardless of whether the prompts are inter-nal or external, this supposition is false. All clinical depressions are a mixture of the emotional and the biochemical; the illness exists some-where in that ghost space between consciousness and chemistry. That is why depressives who are on medication are encouraged, if not re-quired, to also be in therapy.

Reluctantly, I am on medication. I take ten milligrams of Paxil a day. On a number of occasions while I have been in a depression, I have tried to deny my need for medication and stopped taking it. Each time, at the slightest provocation, I have fallen, fast and hard, deeper into the depression. Knowing the physical and psychological anguish that the illness can cause, I am all for whatever works—be it elec-troshock, antidepressant medication, or homeopathy. Still, there is something that seems really wrong with the fact that Prozac is one of the most prescribed drugs in this country. Maybe I just don't want to accept the reality that so many of us are in pain.

"ISOLATION"

MARTHA ELLEN HUGHES

1999

A descendant of early Mississippi settlers, Martha Ellen Hughes grew up in a secretive family that did its best to hide madness. As an isolated yet inquisitive child, she learned about relatives whose mental illnesses were cleverly disguised in elaborate tales. As an adult, she left the South, only to realize that she could not break the powerful emotional ties to her eccentric family. In this essay, Hughes examines the destructiveness of isolation.

To be or not to be mentally ill is not the question in my family. We are all unbalanced and suffer from depression, neuroses, manic behavior, all the way up to schizophrenia. This dirty little secret is the reason, I now think, that the women, especially the women, in my family worked so hard at indoctrinating the children with the idea we were from an old, exceptionally gifted family: We were blue bloods.

I used to love to sit pressed against my grandmother and stare at the blue veins running through her old hands as proof that it was so. Even later, when I was old enough to know better, I was still buying this carefully crafted aristocratic family image.

"Your mother thinks you're descended from Charlemagne," my father said one day when I stumbled upon him alone in the living room engrossed in musical laughter. That day Mama and her cousin had received conclusive proof from a South Carolina genealogist that our family sprang through an illegitimate line from the king of the Franks.

"Charlemagne's horse, more like it," Daddy roared.

I had the guile to laugh, too. What does he know, I thought. A Northerner. From a family careless about losing its members. I was sure my mother and her cousin knew what they were talking about. You can't get more blue-blooded than descending from a king.

Many more years had to pass, the older generation had to die, and I had to veer close to madness myself before realizing what all the talk of aristocracy hid. While it is true that my great-grandfather walked home to ruin from the Civil War and built a fortune before his death in 1906, the kind of money most people in the war-ravaged South could not envision even eighty years later, and true that family members founded towns, started the Mississippi Archives, became writers, doctors, lawyers, mathematicians, ministers, and even allowed its women to attend college in the 1890s, what resounds more are the silent souls left out of the chronicle of the family's splendid accomplishments.

For these I have always felt a great affinity, a hungering to know more. There was Aunt Missouri, named according to the fashion of the day for the most recent state to enter the union, who ran away with a Cherokee and disappeared down the Trail of Tears into Oklahoma. Deemed mad by her blue-blooded kin, her name was still whispered almost a century later.

There was Uncle Isaac Newton, who spent his last meals hoisted in the air by a system of pulleys attached to his chair to keep the ants off the food that dribbled down his chin while he ate. (Who, I want to know, was the madder, Uncle Ike or my cousins who cooked up this plan?) There was my great-uncle, who vanished after leaving a movie to smoke a cigarette. Was he murdered? Did he desert from the navy? Or simply walk off pursued by private demons? I do not even know his name.

It is natural to protect children from unpleasant or frightening stories, to not want them to know about family members who have hurt, perplexed, or disappointed, but there is a level of desperation apparent in my family's pattern of deleting such relatives from the family's collective memory, from its stories told over and over to the children, while filling the gaps left by these omissions with stories glorifying family members we were allowed to know.

This glorification, I now see, served to justify our family's isolation.

The children in our family knew from an early age that we had no need to mix freely with other people; it was more than sufficient to play with our siblings and cousins. And so we did. Or, more correctly, I did; my brother, the oldest child, always felt blamed for the mischief we got into and thus refused prolonged visits to my mother's family in Mississippi, where my beloved grandmother and aunt were the salient purveyors of the family's glory and attendant isolation.

Isolation is dangerous, I now know. It is the hallmark of troubled people, the breeding ground of addictions and mental illness. It is easier to be perverse when one is hidden. People in trouble know there is something wrong with them—that is why they hide.

When the guardians of small children are troubled, keeping the world at bay is not difficult. Once the children enter school, it becomes more problematic, although still not a daunting task. It is fairly easy to isolate children. Find fault with their friends. Nothing flashy. Point out that their friends' parents don't read much, that their mothers don't supervise them enough. Be less than enthusiastic whenever the names of these friends come up. Wonder why they have continual bad colds, complain that they live too far away. Make fun of a mother's new Sunday hat, a father's tendency to talk with his hands. Anything will do.

I know this is how it's done, not because I was smart enough to pick it up, but because years later, I remembered my mother saying that when she was a girl, her mother always found fault with her friends.

Although loneliness and the feeling that I can never quite belong have been hallmarks of my adult life, as a child, I did not feel the isolation much. I was always eager to visit my Mississippi family. I loved playing with my cousins. It seemed then, and does now, a magical time. We were a unit. Four bright, imaginative ⁀ le children playing together on our own in the days before chil ı got carted everywhere by their mothers; there was little of today's supervised play. No television. No excess of toys. The bamboo clumps growing in the back were teepees or castles, depending on the game. A gold-brown scarf cast off by my aunt provided endless hours of Beautiful Ladies, which my girl cousin and I played by passing the scarf back and forth between us. While one tied and retied the scarf, pulled the golden tresses over her shoulder and preened, the other would say, "My, what beautiful hair!" until it was time for the hair to pass back and the other Beautiful Lady to appear. Often while we were thus engaged my cousin Robin, a year older than I, was in the front yard talking to the mint patch growing under the faucet, although he would grow silent when we approached.

I did not find this odd. It seemed dear and typical of our family sensibility: We were special. We lived on a higher plane.

The only times I felt the isolation were when we came up against children our own age—at vacation Bible school, for example, or the town swimming pool, when occasionally some especially sweet girl who attended my cousins' church would break off from her crowd and paddle over a moment to talk but soon seem alarmed and paddled back. I noticed that boys made a game of jumping into the water on top of Robin, so that he came up coughing and frightened. We said nothing, drew closer together in the water, and soon left. Once home, my aunt would rail against the brutes and bullies of the world, of which this Mississippi village of four thousand seemed to have more than its share. We were to watch out for them and come home immediately if threatened. Her fantastical tirade was our only defense.

Most of all, I felt the isolation at the birthday party my aunt gave me every summer. I had always felt my aunt withheld affection from me. That this was done because, in some way, she felt a sort of jealousy on behalf of her own children. I was the oldest granddaughter and, so I thought, the favorite of our grandmother. And yet, in spite of my aunt's withholding, not a summer went by when she did not make a little celebration of and for me. A decorated cake, sometimes even store-bought, in the years when the village had a bakery; flowers on the table; even party decorations and pu ⌐ Then she would make out a guest list, suggesting appropriate nai of children I knew from frequent visits to my cousins' Sunday school class, and I would be permitted to choose.

There was always something wrong about these parties, something old-fashioned, dated. Always an air of strained finances, in the handmade crepe decorations, the party favors she cooked up. She would take out her good silver and china for these affairs, which contributed to the echoing coldness, the stiffness of the celebration.

Girls went to parties then in their nicest Sunday clothes. You were expected to behave and display nice manners. Not grab food, wait until it was offered. Take a present nicely wrapped with a bow and a name tag. At other birthday parties I had attended, we played Pin the Tail on the Donkey with new cardboard donkeys, whereas at my aunt's, we might play Chinese checkers on a mangy-looking board, its colors rubbed off thirty years before by my mother, aunt, and uncle. Or, I could offer my guests croquet, which in all of Mississippi only my family still played.

My aunt would always limit my guest list to one or two girls, with the result that my aunt, two cousins and I outnumbered the guests. The little girls would arrive in their starched dresses, petticoats, and patent leather shoes and, looking very prim and silent, sit in a row on the antique brocade sofa, side by side, hands in laps, eyes cast down, watching us through their lashes. I felt observed, found peculiar, like a wild animal in a zoo.

They were sad little parties. All around the air of great effort to please, the failure hitting me in the face. I wanted so badly for her not to realize this.

And yet, this annual effort my aunt made to celebrate my birth and hers, for she was born at midnight on the same day as I, remains a tender memory of my childhood. My mother did not make much of birthdays or holidays, seemed not to understand the importance of rituals the way my aunt did. Without her, I wonder if I ever would have had a birthday party.

She was a difficult woman. A sometime battle-ax and former schoolteacher. She believed in the eye-for-an-eye kind of justice. She and my female cousin held me down while she instruc ⸱ Robin to spit on me, as punishment for spitting on him. The primi⸱ impulse still shocks me. But those pitiful birthday parties in some odd way bound me to her, despite her harshness, made me respond to her need years later when the tendency to isolate, which had always been there, became absolute.

When Robin was twenty-nine, he was working as a civilian mathematician for the navy. One day, his boss called my aunt and uncle and told them Robin was in the hospital; he had had a breakdown. Eventually, he was diagnosed as schizophrenic, given shock treatments, and, when stable, taken home to live with his parents. This is what many parents do, over the objections of psychiatrists who want the mentally ill to live in group homes, not isolated with their families. My aunt and uncle would not hear of it; it was, they felt, their duty to protect their once brilliant, now troubled son. Robin never left home again.

For the next thirty years, he lived there with his mother, father, and our grandmother, who was showing every sign of living to a great age, until the early 1980s, when one by one members of the family began to die. First went my aunt's husband, then her brother, and her sister three years later; finally, her mother died in 1986. Robin and his mother were then on their own.

From the moment her mother died, my aunt seemed to stoop and shuffle her feet as an old lady would. The sudden change alarmed me; literally overnight, I saw before me my 102-year-old grandmother. My aunt was mimicking her deceased mother's walk.

The ladies in my aunt's Sunday school class must have been alarmed, too. She was only seventy-two, too young to look that way. She had always been tall, erect, and energetic. Now she struggled and gasped for breath to walk from the car to the church door. They began to inquire about her health.

" 'What's wrong with you?' " my aunt would say, bitterly mimicking them. "Oh, I don't say a word back to them," she'd say, her eyes flashing defiance.

Not long after that she gave up going to church entirely. Robin continued to go to church and sing in the choir, but she complained about this a lot, nagging him to stop. When I once asked her why, as Robin's singing in the choir was the one social outlet he had, she told me she was scared for him to drive, he had to tal   ) many drugs. Finally, a doctor in the choir made a rude crack abo   !obin sneezing; he never went back. The walls were closing in.

For a long time after her husband and mother died and she stopped going to church, people my aunt had known all her life would call her on the telephone, sometimes drop by. Robin was always present at these visits. He'd begin by being silent and finish by dominating the conversation in the room. Regardless of what new miracle drug he was on, Robin answered every question exhaustively, speaking so rapidly that all the words ran together, and then he repeated what he'd said again and again. My aunt would grow silent, slump in her chair. The guests would try to be jovial and keep up with his racing, crazed mind, pretending in the Southern way that nothing was amiss. Then everyone in the room would stop trying and Robin would race on, explaining how income taxes should be done, then explaining it again, then starting anew from the same sentence. Sometimes he giggled wildly at jokes he inserted, which nobody could understand. Or sometimes he would riff on a quotation from the Bible, or something in *Scientific American* that had caught his eye. (He was crazy, not stupid, we seemed endlessly to have to explain. He had been a mathematician. A National Merit Scholarship finalist!)

When it became clear that my aunt could not be visited alone, that she would always insist her son be present, her lifelong friends stopped coming. One could hardly blame them. To be with a mentally ill person is often frustrating, boring, and ultimately depressing. "What can I do!" she would cry when I urged her not to include him, at the very least to take a drive alone with me in the car. Anything to buy her an hour of silence, relief from Robin's clattering, machine-gun mouth. How could she stand being locked up with him day and night, never a moment off? I could barely take him an hour.

On the rare occasions she did go, she would cut the drive short, insist on getting back. "Robin will worry," she would say. Or, "Poor thing. I hate to leave him alone."

Her "normal" children felt abandoned by my aunt. "She's my mother, too!" my female cousin complained bitterly when we spoke on the phone. "They're so close, they're like an old married couple. I don't think Robin will outlive her." Finally, alt gh they telephoned their mother each week, she and her brother a topped going to see her.

But I could not stop myself, even though I, too, felt the sense of utter frustration and abandonment my cousin complained about. Twelve years went by in which I traveled from New York to Mississippi three or four times a year, watching her weaken, hearing her angry refusals to walk farther than from her bedroom in the back of the house to the dining room in the front, observing her ever-narrowing world closing in. The trips were expensive; they interrupted my work; I had to be strong to deal with my aunt and cousin, but paid for this strength with depression upon my return. My therapist said the constant trips south prevented me from developing my own life in New York. It made no difference. I continued to go.

I have always been emotionally attached to the South; nothing ever felt so much like home, despite my having lived in the North since I was twenty-two. I could not leave the South behind. This, of course, can be seen as an emotional problem, this unwillingness to get on with life, to grow up. But I always thought it more complicated than that. I had grown up in this odd family, force-fed since infancy with the notion that it was special, that no one could ever take the place of my family. Now one by one they had died. Of the three strong women in my family—my mother, my grandmother, and my aunt—now two were gone; only my aunt remained. My least favorite of the three had now become the surrogate for all the women in my family; through her I could maintain touch with them. She was my mother's "baby sister" and needed my help.

It was hard to arrive and never have her to myself. She hadn't my mother's or grandmother's sense of fun, but her voice and accent were the same; being with her, I could call them up at will. Psychologists say the mind sometimes remembers the good longer than the bad. Certainly I remembered the family picnics, the jaunts through the countryside to pick wild blackberries and plums, the fun we used to have, all the women gathered together in the kitchen before our family's holiday meals, when we all traveled great distances to be together. My aunt rejoiced in remembering, too. There was no one else I could share these memories with. My brother, my cousins, and I were rarely in touch. Robin's memory had been destroyed by shock treatments. The memories he dredged up were obviously bogus, pitiful remnants he repeated endlessly in a vain attempt to believe his memory was intact.

As the years went by, I realized it was more than my sense of duty that kept me going back to see her, more than a feeling of "paying her back" for those long ago summer birthday parties. As odd as it might seem, I admired her, this stooped-over shell of my aunt, pretending to be her mother. She was intelligent. Either despite or because of her eccentricities, she was more of an independent thinker than most people I knew. Although Southern Baptist to the core, she was appalled at the growing conservative movement in the church and the abandonment of its once-proud belief in the separation of church and state. While the rest of the South was enthralled with Ronald Reagan, she saw the mean-spirited politics behind his congenial mask. The cost to her own sanity was apparent, but I admired her determination to provide as much of a normal life for her son as she could. Despite my growing admiration and love, it was never easy to get in the car and drive 1,600 miles, only to arrive and get a fast hug from her and Robin before they retreated into the television, or behind a book or newspaper. Why on earth did I come? I would fume to myself the night of my arrival. They hardly notice I'm here! It finally dawned on me that my aunt did not need rescuing. She had secured her own isolation from the world by using her schizophrenic son as a shield.

I wondered if there were something wrong with me for admiring her. Her behavior was at best self-destructive; to keep him out of mental institutions, she was losing her own grip on reality. She became replete with quirky habits. She had always been afraid of "bogeymen" seeing into her house at night, but now she kept the curtains closed throughout the day, held tight with a bobby pin. The windows were always closed and locked, even in the summertime, and the air conditioners off, as Robin was afraid of electricity.

While dust collected on the china and crystal in her china cabinet, she and Robin ate and drank out of plastic food and yogurt containers, which they carefully washed and collected. Whenever I went home, I would open the kitchen cabinets and find hundreds neatly stacked. When I tried to throw them away surreptitiously while washing up after a meal, Robin would sneak into the kitchen and cry out, "Mama! She's throwing away the yogurt cups again!" Ditto everything else I tried to straighten and clean.

Robin's bedroom was filthy. For years he had been dropping his mail and clothes in the middle of the floor, until only a narrow path wound through the garbage from the door to his bed. When she was stronger, my aunt used to simply close his bedroom door.

"Martha Ellen, I just have to let him do what he wants," was her standard statement to my objections. Despite her growing frailty, her inability to walk or stand for any length of time, my aunt never demanded Robin's help with the house or yard. It was always this lame excuse—she had to let him do what he wanted. Was she afraid of him? At times I certainly was. When pressed to do a task he found odious, this ordinarily sweet, childlike man would grow silent, withdrawn, his face a dark mask.

For the last five years of her life, my aunt sat in her recliner by the curtained front window, often with her hands tucked between her legs. She had beautiful hands—the long, tapered fingers of someone who played the piano and the violin. "My hands!" she used to cry. "I need to do something with my hands! But I've forgotten how to tat!" There was always a reason she could not do something she wanted to do.

Finally, Robin's mess spilled over into the rest of the house. His mail piled up in the dining room, where they always sat during the day, until it spilled over onto the floor. My aunt began to slip and fall on the numerous magazines he ordered. When I would hear of it and call from New York to express concern, she would say, "These old bones are tough, but, oh, you should see my bruise. It goes from my hip to my knee." Then giggle, maddeningly; or was she mad?

Secretive, opinionated, stubborn, she was and always had been a formidable, often irritating woman. But now the fire was gone.

In the spring of 1997, she had a series of strokes. When she was better, her son flew down and took her up North to live temporarily in a nursing home near him and his family. She stayed for three months and came back refreshed. The time away from Robin had restored her; she seemed almost the aunt I knew. But before long, the aberrant behavior began again, or maybe it had never ended. On my next trip home, there were mice droppings on the mail-strewn table where they ate. When I fussed and fumed, my blue-blooded aunt seemed only mildly interested to learn she was eating surrounded by feces.

I went down to visit her in January, in April, and once again in early June. Each time she said as though for the first time, "I keep thinking of how hard we worked to get the few nice things we have, and now, it's come to this. What for? No one wants these big, old antiques. No one has a house or room big enough for them. No one comes to visit anymore. Yes, I've been thinking a lot about that lately."

On that trip in early June, she thanked me for loving her. She wanted to know if I wanted anything. I should have known what that meant. But I am a member of this family, too. I know how to block reality. She died three weeks later.

Robin now lives in an adult assisted-living facility. The house, which my aunt left to him, stands empty; rather, I should say, no one lives there. It is still full of furniture, stacks of mail, the hundreds of little packets of ketchup, duck sauce, soy sauce, sugar, and salt they collected over the years from take-out meals, the yogurt cups and plastic containers, the fabulous crystal and china. Robin has put the house on the market, and I am going to buy it.

"What on earth do you want with that house in Mississippi?" my friends and therapist say.

I have no answer. I suppose I am still taking care of my aunt and the ghosts of all the people I once loved inside that house.

I do wonder about my own sanity, not solely because of buying the house. In my twenties, I, too, had a rough time, a time when I lay in bed all day pretending to be an inanimate object so the angel of death would not notice me. My therapist and drugs pulled me through. She tells me it is natural for children who grow up with a mentally ill sibling or cousin to question their own sanity. But that's not what I am afraid of; I know I am not schizophrenic. As much as I pitied, admired, and finally loved my aunt, I do not want to be like her. Maybe that is the reason I am buying her house. Maybe when I've fixed it up and peopled it with another family, I'll be able to put my family to rest. It is time to stop driving 1,600 miles to find hom

"Thorazine Shuffle"

Allie Light

1999

"I was always so afraid that someone would ask me where I was when JFK was shot, and I would have to say I was in a mental institution," says sixty-four-year-old filmmaker Allie Light. As a young mother immobilized by depression, Light sought treatment at two San Francisco psychiatric hospitals, where she was prescribed an assortment of drugs, group therapy, and volleyball. After becoming a filmmaker, Light revisited her experiences with mental illness as well as those of six other women in her documentary "Dialogues with Madwomen," which won an Emmy Award in 1994. In this essay, she writes about madness as a metaphor.

BREAKDOWN

I was twenty-seven years old when I began having the blues, not feeling in control of my life. I needed help with my children. I was afraid I didn't know how to be a mother. There were no good feelings to balance the down feelings, the depression. This progressed to a feeling of detachment. I remember slicing onions and thinking that my hands were not mine. They appeared to be disc᠎᠎ ᠎cted from my arms, my arms not attached to my body. I had been ᠎᠎᠎ng a doctor and now he prescribed Stelazine, a strong tranquilizer, which, I thought, seemed to be an odd prescription for depression. As my body began to respond to the Stelazine, I experienced extreme feelings of disconnectedness, of being distanced from things. I thought I might hurt my children, I felt like I *was* going to hurt them. I anticipated danger. I began to go to sleep at night with the car keys under my pillow, in case I had to rush the baby to the hospital. I suffered from deep anxiety. One day I put the children in the car to go to my mother's house. I drove through every red light. I could not transfer my foot from the accelerator to the brake, I was too nervous, too leaden, too spasmodic, too jittery. My mother took me to the emergency room where doctors stood around me and watched my legs hammering the air. I could not still my body.

The doctor increased the medication. Somebody was going to fall, somebody was going to be hurt, somebody was going to die. Four o'clock in the afternoon had become an unusual hour. The particular slant of the light, the quality of late afternoon light angled on the hardwood floor, refracted on walls and objects and my senses, urged me to pile my clothes, everything that was mine, onto the floor—precisely in the center—and set them afire. To fight this impulse I would force myself to sleep. To dream through the afternoon, deaf to the voices of my children, my orphans.

On the advice of the doctor, my husband took me to San Francisco General Hospital, where I signed myself into the psychiatric ward. The time was nine o'clock in the evening. While waiting for the doctor, we were seated in a padded cell. The hospital was crowded; there was no other place to wait. The padded cell felt like a diving bell. *I am to be dropped into the depths of the sea.* A doctor finally came, crowding into the space. She was a woman psychiatrist, the first female I had seen in this capacity. She wrote down that I had wanted to burn my clothes at four o'clock. She noted that I had said my children were in peril because "*they couldn't possibly live in this world and, as their mother, it is up to me to do something about that.*" She filled in the papers, and my husband and I walked up the stairs toward the ward, which was called the locked ward. There he left me and went home to take care of the children, and there I went inside and the c   was slammed and locked.

I was asked to remove my clothes and told that I would be examined by a doctor. A drape was given to me to cover the front of my body and I was left waiting alone. After some time the doctor entered and took my medical history. He asked me to lie down on the gurney and he examined my body. He then told me to sit up. He was standing behind me when he said, "*Do you like to kiss your husband's penis?*" I tried to answer him, but I didn't know what to say. My brain was caught in a bind. I thought, If I say no, does that mean that I'm frigid, a bad wife and I hate my husband—and that's my problem? If I say yes, does that mean I'm a nymphomaniac, or a whore, and that's my problem? I lowered my head, ashamed and embarrassed. Trapped. And so, from my tangled tongue, came the reply "*Sometimes.*"

For twenty-five years I've wondered why he asked me that question and if he had any idea how such a question affects a naked woman sitting in a brightly lit room, in the presence of a stranger. What I might do with my husband was not a consideration in my diagnosis. I swear it had nothing to do with the reason I was there, nothing to do with why I should be admitted. That question had only to do with what he wanted to know about me. In my younger life I had often been made to believe there was a quality in me, something about me, that made men behave badly.

HOSPITAL

The first thing I noticed when I was secured on the ward was that, even though the hour was late, people were awake and moving around. There seemed to be two distinct groups—the depressed people like myself and a frenzied population, mercurial in speech and deed. This second group of women, who were in constant motion, running here and there and talking to themselves, had a kind of energy which I had never seen. The room was divided into two battling armies, the depressives and the manics, and it really was a war. I was given something to make me sleep—*I was put to sleep*—and the next morning the war was in full progress.

Immediate existence described life in War ̄ ̄ ? at San Francisco General Hospital in 1963. There was no *after* ̄ *ile,* there was not a plan for *later.* We lived only in the present turmoil. The doctors were shut off in a glass-enclosed area, and the people who actually had contact with us were the "techs"—wading into the crowded ward to break up fights, administer medications, and remove patients who were going home, meeting with their doctors, or violent enough to isolate. The depressed people huddled at one end of the room and the manics ran around frightening everybody to death. My bathrobe was stolen and a woman walked through the door wearing my slippers. Corridors between beds had become spaces for more beds, so people moved sideways in order to pass through. In the corridor at the foot of my bed was jammed another bed, the two forming an upside-down T. The woman in this bed had created the perfect barrier to keep people away. She had outlined her bed on four sides with numerous pieces of toilet tissue. Each wad of tissue was covered with her feces. In the chaos of the ward, she lay alone. Undisturbed. On one side of me a woman sat for an entire day without moving. I never saw her blink once. At night the tech put this statue to bed and, the following day, he again arranged her. The bed to my right held an old, bald woman. I hadn't seen the bedsores that covered her until she turned her back to me. A knit cap she wore to keep her head warm was continually falling off. I remember fishing it from under the radiator behind her bed and stretching it over her head as she slept. This woman's hat reminded another woman of the day she lost her hat on San Francisco Bay. She was sailing with her fiancé and her hat blew off. She watched it float away. The year was 1906.

And then there were the women in perpetual motion: they paced, lurched, fled. Some moved like sleepwalkers, somniferous in their tranquillity; others were propelled by rages, by the snare of waking dreams unfolding before them. These women did not see us, did not hear us. The voices they heard were not ours, yet they flung themselves upon us. I was stalked by the cocoa spitter. She saved her nightly cocoa for me. She watched me and she followed me, cup in hand. I could keep her at bay with my eyes, but if I looked away, she was immediately in my face, spraying me with cocoa from her mouth or flicking it at me with her fingers—throwing 'y drops each time, measuring her supply. I had become so undif ntiated, permeable, that these hopeless women seemed like aspects of myself. They—we—were acting out parts of our lives that we had once lived through, or could not live through.

After a few days I adapted to this life. I learned how to hang on to my possessions or how to recover them when they were taken from me. When they were not on my body or in my mouth, I kept my bathrobe, slippers, and toothbrush under the mattress. I sat on them. They were mine.

Eventually a bed became available for me at Langley Porter, the psychiatric facility at UC San Francisco. I was finished with Stelazine and Librium. At Langley Porter, Thorazine was the drug of choice.

DR. SCHWARTZ

Langley Porter was a serfdom. Doctors came in as trainees and we became their property. They moved on as psychiatrists, but we stayed on the land. We were owned by a feudal system that grew and fed on our nightmares, our fantasies, our proclivities to stumble or to drown. Even as these potentates profited from the shambles of our lives, we trusted them.

I was given to Dr. Schwartz. He took care of me, wrote my prescriptions, made sure I took my medication, and was responsible for writing my records. I would see him once or twice a week for therapy. I had been assigned to the day ward for three months, which meant that as long as I stayed on medication and behaved myself, I could sleep at home each night.

Our contract began with the removal of my clothes. Each psychiatrist must give his patient a complete physical exam to rule out factors or conditions that might have an organic cause. Once the body work was out of the way, other evaluations were pursued. I took psychological tests; I drew pictures of my gender. Draw a woman: a stick figure with football shoulders and small, wavy breasts. I was adjusting to Thorazine, which may have been why I forgot to give her a face. With Thorazine came Cogentin, a drug that causes blurred, even double, vision. Now there were two reasons I could not read. I couldn't concentrate and I couldn't see.

I had entered a kindergarten of managed play. We had activities— occupational therapy, volleyball, pool. The physical therapists pressed upon us the need to practice looking beautiful. With our uncombed hair and unfocused vision, we sleepwalked the corridors with books on our heads to improve our postures. We had group therapy, a macabre version of Show and Tell. There were field trips to a bowling alley, to a park where we rented bicycles and tried to pedal and steer while sodden with Thorazine, Mellaril, Lithium, Haldol, Elavil, Tofranil, Miltown.

Some activities were less benign; we were once seated, one at a time, in an enclosed cockpit where a panel of lights was set a few inches from our faces. The lights were different colors and set to strobe at different speeds. The effect was one of continual flashbulbs exploding through the eyes and into the brain. Even after they slapped a wet towel on my face, I couldn't stop screaming.

A mental patient was not allowed to refuse medication. We were warned to "take it orally or it will be injected." I felt terrible on Thorazine. I was deathly afraid of the medication and once it was in my system I experienced extreme anxiety combined with difficulty in walking, moving, thinking, staying awake—the drug is designed to imprison the body. With each dose, I expected to die and so before I swallowed a capsule I would plead to the nurse, "*Do you have oxygen here? Can you do CPR? Once I take this and I begin to die, can you save me? Will you bring me back to life?*" And she would encourage me, "You'll be all right, you're going to be OK." Thorazine had this strangling effect on me. I fell into blackness and the return was a murky swim toward sound and light. The final time Thorazine was forced upon me was post-Schwartz. I was unconscious for two days. After the injection I had tried to rise and, instead, had fallen to the floor. I felt the doctor's fingers pushing against my eyelids, checking the pupils of my eyes. He told me later that I now had a warning posted in my records—that I would not be given Thorazine again. There is no way a patient, using her own words, can logically convince a doctor that she knows something about her person. He has to see for himself and then, if the patient doesn't die, she might have won her poin

I always had the feeling that Dr. Schwar   'as memorizing his lessons prior to our appointments, but I pretended not to know because I wanted him to make me well. I sat facing him and he would ask me, "What does 'A rolling stone gathers no moss' mean?" I knew about allegory and figurative speech, but this was insulting and I didn't want to play. Each time he asked for a metaphor, I gave him the literal meaning. *Nothing can grow on a stone that is moving.* I would never look at him. I kept my eyes averted. He continually urged me to make eye contact. He said I would feel better if I looked at him. I always glanced away when I spoke because I didn't think I had interesting things to say. I finally decided that I would try. I told myself that I was going to be very direct and I would look right into his eyes. I practiced for a week by choosing a spot on the wall and silently addressing Dr. Schwartz, my eyes riveted to this mark that was his face. My hour of therapy came and I said, as I entered the room, "Today I feel like I can talk to you and I'm going to look at you when I speak." I spoke to him and I stared into his eyes. Suddenly I said, "I want you to know that I . . . that I love you." I said this to him and I did not break eye contact. About four seconds passed before he replied, "Well, you don't have to look so *long!*"

I obeyed Dr. Schwartz. I wanted to be a good girl and I thought his job was to make me well, so I would do whatever that entailed. He began to give me assignments. The first one was that I could go home on the weekend if I would bake a turkey. So I went home and baked a turkey. The second week the assignment was that I mop all the floors in my house. I mopped every floor. And I thought to myself, "Maybe I'm getting better. This is making me better." I often told Dr. Schwartz that I needed something in my life. I desired something of my own. I wanted to be somebody. I said that I wanted to go to school; I could be the first person in my family to graduate from college. His reply to me was, "If you can't stay home and take care of your children, then get a job. Don't waste everyone's time by going to college."

One afternoon Dr. Schwartz and I were coming back from a therapy session. We were walking down the hall, just about to enter the ward, when a young man, another patient, came running toward us. He was agitated, frantic, frenzied, and he   ried the receiver end of the wall telephone in his hand. He had jer   it off the wall. When he saw Dr. Schwartz, he began to shout, "The president is dead. He's been killed. The president has been shot." Dr. Schwartz turned to me and said, "Don't pay any attention to him, he's just hallucinating." And that was the assassination of John F. Kennedy. At that moment Dr. Schwartz would have preferred to change the course of history rather than admit to being wrong. To justify their work, must psychiatrists believe that what comes out of the mouths of their patients is not real? If so, then *they* hallucinate.

At the close of three months there was to be a dance party. For me. I was going home. Langley Porter's version of the lunatics' ball was a dance that fell between a 1950s prom night and a Thorazine shuffle. We were like zombies traipsing around to old records of Johnnie Ray singing "The Little White Cloud That Cried." The grandest event that could befall a female patient was to dance with her psychiatrist. And so I danced with Dr. Schwartz. We were completely out of step. We pretended that we were not patient and doctor. That this was *not* a mental hospital. But there is no way you can go to a prom on Thorazine and think that you are anyplace else.

MADNESS

Mental illness in women was once thought to be caused by a floating womb. A womb bobbing around inside like a cork. And how does a man become mentally ill *without* a womb?

Depression is not about pain. Depression is about the absence of pain, the absence of feeling. Depression covers anxiety and fear like a fog. Once depressed, I was no longer anxious about my children. If I drank a cup of coffee, my mood was not enhanced; if I went to a party, I didn't feel better. If I read poetry, my soul no longer blossomed as it had in the past. *No feeling* is what depression is about, and the condition created a barrier between me and my children, my husband, my friends. Depression is not about pain: it's about everything gone away.

I come from a line of women who endured depression. They passed their sufferings on to their daughters. My grandmother gave birth to nine children—a child every two yea Her despair at perpetual pregnancy was contagious. My mothe s a small girl when her mother tried to hang herself from the kitchen rafters. Pregnant again. My mother carried stories such as this one to her own children. Her mission in life was to frighten me to death. I died over and over. By the time I was four years old my nightmares were fraught with pictures of Bluebeard's dead wives hanging from the ceiling—the blood on the key proof that the lock had been turned, the door opened; and Edgar Allan Poe's women sealed in walls with cats on their shoulders, or buried alive, their fingernails and hair continuing to grow. Even Psyche had become a murderous wench, pouring hot wax on the sleeping Eros.

My mother was compelled to tease until my brother and I cried. She would play dead on the floor and we could not awaken her. She turned off the lights and crawled toward us, a huge animal growling and shuffling, backing us into the corners of the room. Her favorite bedtime story was about the little girl who was afraid of being stolen from her bed. The child's mother got into bed with her and tied a string from her toe to the child's toe, so she would wake if the child was taken. *She promised her little girl she would be safe.* The man came into the house, he came up one stair, he came up two stairs, he came up three stairs, and when he stole the girl from her bed, the string broke, the mother slept on, and the girl was never found. I was probably the only child in kindergarten who knew well the literature of blood, gore, suffocation, and death.

The stories told to me by my mother were about the consequences one paid for looking: Because the blood would not wash off the key, the new wife could not hide the fact that she had unlocked the door and looked at the dead wives. Psyche lost her lover for looking at him with a lighted candle. She had been bidden to love in the dark. One is punished for her gaze. "*Don't stare*," the mother says to her little girl. Women in each generation of my family endured lives of poverty; they passively suffered the births of many children, yet they knew there were other lives they could have lived. *They were afraid to look.*

And what did I learn from my mother's stories? At an early age I learned that things stand for other things. The bloody key stood for the fact that I could not return to a state ˜ blindness. I have had to look at my life. And I have escaped from   dness by understanding transformation, how each thing transcends its own reality.

I either go mad or I learn about metaphor.

"A Better Place to Live"

MAUD CASEY

2001

At age eighteen, Maud Casey suffered a manic episode that landed her in a psychiatric hospital for six weeks. Diagnosed with manic-depression, she began taking medication and slowly emerged from her harrowing experience. Her recovery stayed intact for a decade, until she tried discontinuing her lithium. She was hospitalized again—this time for two months. "A Better Place to Live" chronicles Casey's discoveries about the role of family in battling mental illness. The author of a novel and a short-story collection, Casey now teaches Creative Writing.

It's March 1999, two months since I stopped wishing I was dead. I read my mother's journal as I ride the F train to the end of the line in Queens—179th and Hillside—to the psychiatric hospital where I spent most of last summer due to manic-depression. Surprisingly—as I come from a family of relentlessly nosy writers who believe anything not under lock and key is free game—I have my mother's permission to read her journal that spans my hospitalization and the five-month depression that consumed me after my discharge. I am doing research, trying to find out what the ex〉   ᵊnce of my depression was like for other people. After my relea   ʳom the hospital—once I no longer believed that the hospital staff was training a twenty-four-hour surveillance camera on me in order to eventually kill me—I was supposedly ready for the world. But was it ready for me? This is no saintly investigation, no purely altruistic walk in other people's shoes. The subject is still very much me, me, me.

Now that my depression has started to lift, I'm suffering from what I've come to think of as the hangover of the depressed: shame. I crawl out of bed some mornings like someone who has just woken up from a bender. I look in the mirror and think: Oh God, I did *that?* Who saw me? Maybe they won't remember; maybe they were really depressed, too?

This train ride is penance. My mother's journal is balanced on top of my own notebook, which teeters precariously on one knee. I—a former small-town girl who frequently falls *up* stairs and certainly no expert subway-riding-drinker-of-coffee—have a pen in one hand, a sloshing cup of coffee in the other, and the inevitable happens: I spill the coffee all over my mother's journal and the crotch of my pants. The man next to me rolls his eyes and moves away, wanting no part of this, but the woman across the aisle digs Kleenex out of her purse and hands them to me, shaking her head at the chaos in my lap but smiling sympathetically like someone who frequently finds herself cleaning up other people's messes. Above her head is an ad for Maple Gardens, a private rental community with a twenty-four-hour manned gatehouse. There are festive pictures of people in bright clothing playing golf, chatting poolside, and jogging cheerfully on treadmills. "You can't find a better place to live," the caption reads. I wipe the coffee from my mother's words: *I feel Maud's misery and fear packed inside my senses. I wake in terror, always close to tears at dawn.*

I spent the fall of this year, and into winter, sleeping with my mother. In my Dial-A-Mattress bed in Brooklyn, I clung to her, often wrapping an arm, heavy and dead as my gone life, around her waist. I inhaled deeply her scent like smelling salts bringing me briefly back into the world. My mother worked full-time as a documentary filmmaker in New York, rushed to Prospect Heights to cook dinners I would otherwise skip, and traveled back and forth between New York and her home in Illinois. I tried to absorb that energy, her life force, like a plant absorbs the sun. But I wasn't the pure. There was desperation in my clinging—a kind of *Invasion of the Body Snatchers* life-draining suck and I had become pure suck, the alien pod.

September 8, 1998: Sleeping with Maud in her bed. The feeling both of laying my motherhood at her disposal and being a sponge to her deep fears and despair. The moon beams down on her through the window. I often think of her child body, child self, the joy she brought, how fascinated we were by everything she did; her stately, majestic, orderly procession through her skills and speech and school. These images return to me now as premonitions of pain to come. I look at her darling baby child self as wounded, as shrinking, shriveling in the shadows of her future suffering. Yet when I wake up at night, my child (a twenty-nine-year-old woman, but childlike in her pajamas, in her petiteness, in her funny little haircut and the simple sound of her breathing) is still there, my Maud bathed in the moonlight.

During the weeks my mother spent in Illinois, my sister would sleep over on occasional nights. In her white nightgown with lace fringe around the neck, she was a radiant beauty—a successful writer and magazine editor who had recently fallen in love. She was my fairy-tale princess and my tentacles slithered out of their alien pod, wrapping themselves around her.

"I want to go back to the hospital," I would whisper to my mother trying to sleep next to me. "I want to die." "I want to go home," I would say to my sister as she rolled over to hold my shaking hands. The three—hospital, death, home—became interchangeable. "Tell me what's going on," my mother would whisper back, her warm body charged and ready like a nightlight, glowing with the possibility of emergency. "Maybe you could move to Virginia, live in Dad's extra apartment," my sister would offer. And for a minute that would seem like the answer—if only it were possible for me to move and simultaneously leave myself behind in Brooklyn. Unfortunately, to be depressed is not to have words to describe it, is not to have words at all, but to live in the gray world of the inarticulate, where nothing takes shape, nothing has edges or clarity. A literal home was not what I meant.

Home was what my grandmother seemed to talking about in the last months of her life. Here on the train, eighteen different combinations of antipsychotics, mood-stabilizers, and antidepressants later, I remember this. As my grandmother lay dying in the house she shared with her husband in South Hamilton, Massachusetts, she talked a lot about "going home." Would you like something to eat? Some water? More covers? Do you need to go to the bathroom? Her children and husband asked her these questions and she replied with stern practicality, "No, thank you, I'm going home." (In my version of the story, my grandmother wags her long, thin finger satirically at the asker, the way she always did to indicate that underneath her scolding, stern practicality was an appreciation for the naughtiness of the world.) For my grandmother, home was not in South Hamilton anymore. Home wasn't even in her body. She couldn't be bothered with the mundane details of the living—all of this eating, drinking, keeping warm, going to the bathroom, getting up, lying down, staying awake, going to sleep. Home was elsewhere, in death.

In the blackout drunk of depression, home was elsewhere for me, too. Not in my apartment in Brooklyn where I felt like a guest in someone else's falling-apart life—unanswered phone calls, unopened mail, rotting fruit on top of the refrigerator, and something unidentifiable and reeking inside, piles of dirty dishes, tumbleweeds of dust, books I didn't remember reading, furniture I couldn't remember buying, pictures of friends and family that seemed to belong to a stranger. Not in my father's extra apartment. Not in my mother's house in Illinois. Not under my psychiatrist's desk where I wanted to curl up and hide, resting my head on his sensible shoes. Not on my therapist's couch, waiting and waiting for, as Freud put it so succinctly, neurotic suffering to become everyday misery. Not in my body. Not in eating, drinking, keeping warm. Not going to the bathroom or lying down. Not in staying awake or going to sleep. Above the Kleenex woman's head, the glaring reds, nuclear yellows, and shocking blues of the Maple Gardens ad run together in a perky smear. Being depressed felt like living in a corpse, so being dead seemed like "a better place to live."

The depression that follows mania is rarely dealt with as aggressively as the mania itself. Once the hard throb of emergency is over, the presenting crisis passed, many people ʼ left to deal with a depression that leaves them nostalgic for wild, bucking panic of mania—in my case, all those revolutions to tend to, bombs to dismantle (in a moment of unintended irony, I called 911 from the hospital), all those actors playing my friends and family. This hospital is really a whorehouse fronting for a drug cartel, isn't it? No, come on, you can tell me. It is, right?

During my depression, I often thought of something a secretary once said to me as she explained my duties as a temp, leading me through a fluorescent-lit office with no windows where I was to spend the next few months. It's not hard, she said, but it makes you want to shoot yourself. The lifetime risk of suicide among manic-depressives is 10 to 15 percent. Every morning before I went to work as an administrator in a theater school (a job I managed to keep despite all of my efforts to quit—my incredibly patient and kind boss wisely told me I should hang on until my medication had been worked out), my mother and her girlfriend counseled me, in person or over the phone. I can't go, I would say. I can't leave my apartment. I can't get dressed. I can't take a shower. Take a shower, they would say. Put on your clothes—remember your favorite black pants? The green sweater you bought when you first moved to New York? Find your wallet. Your keys. Walk out the door and lock it behind you. Buy a seven-day Metrocard, they would say (*because you can last that long,* they meant). Get on the 2 train, switch to the 4 at Nevins, and ride it all the way to Union Square.

Once I'd made it to work, I made lists: pills, suffocation, subway, bus, cut my wrists. I was forever staring at the tender blue veins along the inside of my wrists, fragile twigs trapped under ice. "Whatever happens, promise me you won't kill yourself," my best friend pleaded. "If you commit suicide, I'll kill you," my mother told me.

September 21, 1998: Everything we worked for gone. She's slipped from being a high-functioning, promising, her-whole-life-ahead-of-her-young-woman to being someone beginning a downward grind. We'll have to take her home as a kind of second-class citizen.

When my father's twenty-seven-year-old godson shot himself, it had seemed to me like the mysterious act of a 〔 〕n-up who had seen things that I, at the age of eleven, hadn't. But 〔 〕 then I knew those mysterious things might be waiting for me, and when I was two years older than he would ever be, I could understand the general impulse: Let me out of here! Let me out of this body! I want to go home! But then there was my father visiting me for the day, reduced to tears by my own self-hatred. "I have nothing to say because I don't have any thoughts in my head anymore," I told him over and over. And my mother busting into one of my therapy sessions, a maternal terrorist, demanding that my therapist convince me to stay at my job, that she force me to understand that I didn't actually want to go back to the hospital. "She'll go back to that hospital over my dead body!" And my sister's voice over the phone, stripped of its usual joyousness, smooth and basic as the bone it had become: "Do you know how horrible the hospital was for you? For all of us?" I limited myself to banging my head against the wall, pinching and scratching my twiggy veins for relief.

Trapped in the dead body of depression, I was able to find relief in touch—the touch of friends and family who wanted to keep me from hurting myself as well as from the pain I inflicted on myself. As I clung to my job at the theater school, an institution steeped in the Method, I found myself using the same sense memory—an exercise that allows an actor to create reality through the memory of touch, taste, sight, sound, and smell in the otherwise imaginary circumstances of an empty stage—that I described to potential students during interviews. A childhood friend—her mother lying in a hospital in Virginia after a near-fatal accident—came to *my* apartment and tickled *my* arm, stroked *my* hair as I stood mutely grateful. Her touch reminded me of the power of wordless physical connection, of what I would lose if I died.

One night, my best friend from college, disappointed that I had returned from the hospital (where she visited almost every day) not closer to her but farther away, convinced me to have dinner with her at a loud, clattery restaurant rather than rush home to sleep. We sat opposite each other on long benches shared by other people, including a new crooning couple next to us feeding each other noodles. My friend told me she wasn't sure what to do anymore, that she didn't know how to help me. Why wasn't I calling her? W   vasn't I sleeping on her couch, watching videos and letting her coc   e dinner? I started to cry for the first time in months, relieved at the way her words shot through my medicine haze like a needle into my heart. As we held hands across the table, the anonymous buzz of people talking and laughing around us and our noodle-sharing neighbors oblivious, I remembered the specificity of friendship and was glad to be able to offer her my tears.

Sleeping next to the live bodies of my mother and my sister reminded me that I, too, had been alive once.

October 3, 1998: I am completely braced to do whatever necessary to bring Maud through. I have the clearest feeling of being supported by recent years of happiness (lest anyone mistake me for a selfless person). Packed with satisfaction and strength, I've lived out a lot of things I wanted to do so that it's possible for me to be at her disposal. This feeling pours out for the most part (with occasional moments of self-pity), I will lay my fat years at the service of her lean one. I have a sense of the depth of the emergency. A visual image of the hollow beneath her.

I put my mother's journal and my own notebook into my bag and stand in my coffee-soaked pants to look at the subway map. The Kleenex woman looks up from her book with a momentary flash of concern but then returns to her reading. She's got her own destination. One hundred and seventy-ninth and Hillside is three stops away. In my head, I say the names of the people who rode this train to visit me: Jane B., Janet, Nell, Julia G., Jeremy, Lorraine, Alex, Annie, Jacob, Dwight, Cree, Sofia, Lenore, Rick, Daniel, Rose, Matilda, Molly, Caitlin, Linda T., Steve, Connie, Harold, Helen, Olivia, Virginia, Mike, Bliss, Jan. This list is like an incantation, a poem I have memorized. I have filled entire pages with these names, afraid afterward that I've left someone out and afraid of the list itself, which still has the capacity to split me wide open with humiliation. Like someone who tells her most secret of secrets as she dances naked and drunk in front of everyone she knows, I can never be exactly sure what I revealed. Then there are those who called, who wrote, who saw: John, Ros, Clare, Julia C., Johnny, Lydia, Craig, Linda B., Van, Bruce, Tim, Meredith, Jesse, Tracey, Darcey, Jane H., Tammy, Benjamin, ̄ ̈ ̦, Eve, Nava, Meg, Carolyn H., Nancy, Pat, Victoria, Anna, Caro ̦ T., Thomas, Elizabeth. I can't remember them all. If I could only name all of them I might gain some control over what otherwise feels like a stadium full of people who witnessed this moment of skinlessness. We are at the end of the line.

Hillside Avenue is a grim strip of discount electronic stores and check-cashing places. Discarded fast-food wrappers and sheaves of newspaper blow chaotically down the street. While my mother was in New York taking care of me, she became obsessed with the everyday trash that found its way into the streets.

November 11, 1998: The streets are flooded with litter but most people have washed and dressed themselves in clean clothes. They pick their way through garbage, as if they had nothing to do with it. People make their way along the junky street, transcending the plastic wrap, wax paper, underwear, intent on getting to the office, to their apartment. This morning, when Maud opens her eyes, she is restless and burning with self-hatred and fear. I can't, I'm stupid, I'm not able, no memory. She looks at me and says: You look nice. You're dressed as if there is nothing wrong.

I stand in front of Liquor World and an offtrack betting parlor next to a group of teenagers—two boys and a girl. One of the boys is describing how the girl he went out with last night was so mad tight that it took him half an hour to get three fingers inside of her. I flag a car and read from the tiny, coffee-splattered piece of paper on which I've scrawled the directions: *Hillside to Palo Alto, 1 block to hospital.* (I don't remember the trip here the first time—another childhood friend, whose brother had also been hospitalized, bravely and selflessly escorted me.) Hospital, home, death. I am finally going back to this place I'd claimed I wanted to return. As we pull into the circular drive of the hospital, a woman as thin as the sharp edge of a road sign stands outside smoking a cigarette. She seems familiar—it's as though we could be related. But the context comes back to me. She's one of the mental-health workers who held me down while I was being restrained.

"Hi," she says, stubbing her cigarette out on the hospital windowsill. "How are you?"

"I'm fine," I say. "Well, pretty good. Okay, I guess. You know, all right. So-so." What am I doing? I'm not wearing the right coat for this windy day and I've lost yet another pair of gloves. I want something from this woman. I want her to take me back. Wrested from the land of the living, I imagine myself sleeping the heavy sleep of sadness all day long—skipping groups, never changing out of my pajamas, and re-

ceiving only patients, like-minded people who understand best the
desire to disappear from the face of the earth, as I lie in my sterile,
white, clean hospital bed running a salon for the insane. I want to go
to a place where strangers take care of me, people whose pores are
sealed, filled with their own rotten suffering. But I know better than
that even before I walk back through the doors. Morning meds are at
8:00 A.M., if you aren't dressed you are put on constant supervision,
patients aren't allowed in other patients' rooms, and there are no such
things as sterile, white, clean beds in a psychiatric hospital. At this hospital, you're lucky to get a pillowcase. Saying I wanted to go back to
the hospital was akin to holding a gun to my head.

> *December 3, 1998:* I am hanging on by a thread. I want Maud to hang on to
> her apartment and her job, to stay in the world as proof that she isn't going
> to be ground down, smashed by her depression or marginalized, one of
> those cousins who Aunt Dora used to include at family holidays out of
> kindness. Don't forget—often these terrifying, destabilized events occur
> and you are completely on your own with no idea how to proceed even
> with people around you. What are analogous stories? Having a baby?

Saying I wanted to go back to the hospital was like waving a gun
around at everyone I loved.

Still, I try again. "I want to speak with someone about attending
outpatient groups," I tell the security guard sitting at the front desk.
He is a huge and grouchy man who doesn't look up from the screens
in front of him, screens filled with the threatening stillness of empty
corridors.

"Take a seat," he says.

My former psychiatrist—a jumpy, handsome man with a ponytail
that serves as a barometer for his nerves—bu   out of his office on
the first floor. His ponytail swings wildly bel   him. He scans the
room, sees me, and, being a man trained to head directly for trouble, heads my way. "What are you doing here?" he asks. He thinks I'm
back.

For a minute I consider turning myself over to him, telling him I
want to hurt myself so that he will be forced to act on my behalf. But

shame burns through me like acid, and instead I say something about outpatient groups. He looks me up and down. "For you?" he asks incredulously. "For you to *participate* in?" He asks me about my current psychiatrist, my latest drug cocktail, whether I'm employed, where I'm living. I answer him—smart and kind, Tegretol, Wellbutrin, Effexor, yes, Brooklyn—leaving out the rest, the parts that hover between the facts, such as how I can't figure out how to live in the world after preparing to give up for so long, how I'd gone to the edge and thrown all of my tools over, how the choices involved with living overwhelm me, how I just need to lie down on the old unit and rest for a little while until I feel ready to move back into my body. But he is shaking my hand, congratulating me, and then he sails off, his ponytail a wiggly rudder steering him onto the next crisis.

The grouchy security guard, his eyes still glued to the screens offering a filtered reality easier to bear, buzzes me through doors onto a locked unit so that I can use the bathroom. I go into a stall, sit on the toilet, and weep because I am not welcome here. They won't take me back. I cry mostly because this wasn't the place I'd been wishing for all along. Because what I really wished for was to disappear, and for the first time I see the tragedy of this as clearly as if I was the person lying terrified in my bed next to me or desperately trying to reach me across the table in a crowded restaurant. I cry briefly, efficient as the cold white tiles of the bathroom floor, and then walk back into the lobby where my psychiatrist hovers over a woman and her panicked daughter gesturing wildly. I call a car and go out into the cold gray day to wait. As I stand there, another psychiatrist, the man who performed my intake, strolls up the semicircle of the driveway. He recognizes me vaguely with the wary smile of a man who has seen thousands of patients come and go. I might have been his patient ten years ago or two weeks ago.

"How are you?" he asks, still moving tov   the door. He knows just how much he can afford to give.

"Okay," I say, definitively.

He's partly through the door when, without breaking stride, he says, "It's cold out here." Exactly. He feels it, too. It's cold out here for everybody.

The car doesn't come for another half an hour. I wait alone in my too-thin coat and think about calling my sister when I get back to Brooklyn. Recently, she sent me an essay by Lauren Slater on depression. At first, I was unable—unwilling?—to learn about my own disease. It was mine, all mine! The idea of sharing, the idea of hope, seemed cruel. I had read Kay Redfield Jamison's *An Unquiet Mind* twice, and took a stab at William Styron's *Darkness Visible,* but they left me feeling even more depressed. How was I, a not-yet-published writer who didn't have the energy to turn on her computer, supposed to feel better by reading the stories of depressed, famous writers? But, when I finally came back to myself, remembering how often reading had saved my life, I sat down with the Slater essay.

In the margins of the copy my sister had sent me—the copy she had intended to keep for herself—there were notes scribbled in her familiar, spidery handwriting. My therapist would probably remind me that there are no accidents, but, frankly, this can be an exhausting concept. I *wanted* to see. *Maud's second breakdown and later depression broke my heart in a way I'd never known, a loss that even now, with her back and healthy, I can feel occasionally.* When I could breathe again, I began to see that the cruelty was not so much in the idea of sharing or the idea of hope as it was lodged in the layer of depression that is selfishness. My depression was not all mine, and as I read my sister's words again and again, relief loosened my relentless grip on my illness even as my heart broke, too.

When I call my sister, I won't tell her about this trip to the hospital. Not yet, I want to wait until the story is a gift and not a burden. Instead, I will tell her about a dream I had the other night in which we were the adults we are now wandering through my grandmother's Rhode Island house—a converted barn with beautiful high ceilings and an enormous window overlooking Narrag tt Bay. The Barn, as it was called by our family, no longer exists. My grandmother sold it, and in a perfect symbolic gesture of resistance to its new owners, it burned to the ground. In the dream, my sister and I wander in my grandmother's garden and we come upon myself as a child, pudgy and tan all over from never wearing clothes. We squeeze my squishy child legs and then my child self tells us she's happy. But my sister doesn't hear and my child self runs away, turns into one of the groundhogs that plagued my grandmother by biting the heads off her petunias, and scurries toward the bay. I decide to leave out the part about my child self and just tell my sister about visiting the Barn, how beautiful it was in the sepia tones of dream memory, how blissful it was to wander in the long-ago garden with her.

I check my wallet for carfare and pick the trash—gum wrappers, pens that don't write, paper clips—out of my bag. These mundane details of the living make up the sweet straitjacket of practicality that holds me to the earth. In my mind, I wander through my Brooklyn apartment, where the dishes are done and the floors swept, looking for my gloves—the fifth pair I've lost this winter. I'll find them when I get home.

Notes About the Contributors

Maud Casey is the author of the novel *The Shape of Things to Come* (2001) and a short-story collection, *Drastic* (2002).

Elizabeth Cochrane is the author of *Ten Days in a Mad-House, or Nellie Bly's Experience on Blackwell's Island* (1887), *Six Months in Mexico* (1888), and *Nellie Bly's Book: Around the World in Seventy-two Days* (1890).

Meri Nana-Ama Danquah is the author of numerous poems and essays and *Willow Weep for Me* (1998). She is the editor of *Becoming American: Personal Essays by First Generation Immigrant Women* (2001).

Dorothea Dix is the author of *Conversations on Common Things* (1824), *Hymns for Children* (1825), *Evening Hours* (1825), *Meditations for Private Hours* (1828), and *The Garland of Flora* (1829).

Zelda Fitzgerald is the author of numerous stories and essays, *Save Me the Waltz* (1932), and *Scandalabra: A Farce Fantasy in a Prologue and Three Acts* (1933).

Janet Frame is the author of poetry, several short-story collections, a three-volume autobiography, and the novels *Owls Do Cry* (1957), *Faces in the Water* (1961), *The Edge of the Alphabet* (1962), *Scented Gardens for the Blind* (1963), *The Adaptable Man* (1965), *A State of Siege* (1966 ⁓e *Rainbirds* (1968), *Intensive Care* (1970), *Daughter Buffalo* (1972), *Living in t ˈaniototo* (1979), *The Carpathians* (1988), and *Snowman Snowman: Fables and Fantasies* (1993).

Charlotte Perkins Stetson Gilman is the author of "The Yellow Wallpaper" (1892), *In This Our World* (1893), *Women and Economics* (1898), *Concerning Children* (1900), *The Home* (1903), *Human Work* (1904), *What Diantha Did* (1910), *The Crux* (1911), *Moving the Mountain* (1911), *His Religion and Hers* (1923), and *The Living of Charlotte Perkins Gilman* (1935).

SIGNE HAMMER is the author of three nonfiction books: *By Her Own Hand: Memoirs of a Suicide's Daughter* (1991), *Passionate Attachments: Fathers and Daughters in America Today* (1981); and *Daughters and Mothers: Mothers and Daughters* (1975). In 1975, she also edited a collection of essays, *Women: Body and Culture: Essays on the Sexuality of Women in a Changing Society*. Hammer is currently working on a novel.

MARTHA ELLEN HUGHES is the author of *Precious in His Sights* (1989) and two books of nonfiction. A former newspaper reporter, her work has appeared in *Cosmopolitan*. She founded the Peripatetic Writing Workshop and Colony, Inc., in 1991. Hughes lives in New York City, where she is a freelance book editor and teaches writing at New York University.

SUSANNA KAYSEN is the author of *Asa, As I Knew Him* (1987), *Far Afield* (1990), *Girl, Interrupted* (1993), and *The Camera My Mother Gave Me* (2001).

MARGERY KEMPE is the author of *The Book of Margery Kempe* (1436).

MAXINE HONG KINGSTON is the author of numerous stories and articles, *The Woman Warrior: Memoirs of a Girlhood Among Ghosts* (1976), *China Men* (1980), *Hawaii One Summer* (1987), *Tripmaster Monkey: His Fake Book* (1988), *To Be the Poet (the William E. Massey, Sr. Lectures in the History of American Civilization)* (2002), and *The Fifth Book of Peace* (2003).

ALLIE LIGHT writes, directs, and produces documentary films with her partner, Irving Saraf. She won the 1994 Emmy Award for "Dialogues with Madwomen" and the 1991 Academy Award for Best Documentary Feature for "In the Shadow of the Stars." She has published a book of poems, *The Glittering Cave* (1974), and edited an anthology of women's writings, *Poetry From Violence* (1976). Light also lectured for ten years in the Women Studies Program at San Francisco State University. In 2000, she collaborated with Saraf and Julia Hilder on the documentary *Blind Spot: Murder by Women*.

KATE MILLETT is the author of *Sexual Politics* (1970), *Flying* (1974), *The Prostitution Papers* (1976), *Sita* (1977), *The Basement: Med. ˙ ns on a Human Sacrifice* (1979), *Going to Iran* (1982), *The Loony-Bin Trip* (19   *The Politics of Cruelty: An Essay on the Literature of Political Imprisonment* (1994), *A.D.: A Memoir* (1995), and *Mother Millett* (2001).

ELIZABETH PARSONS WARE PACKARD is the author of *The Exposure on Board the Atlantic & Pacific Car of the Emancipation for the Slaves of Old Columbia, … or, Christianity and Calvinism Compared* (1864), *Great Disclosure of Spiritual*

Wickedness!! In High Places (1865), *Marital Power Exemplified in Mrs. Packard's Trial, . . . or, Three Years' Imprisonment for Religious Belief* (1866), and *Modern Persecution, or Insane Asylums Unveiled* (1873).

SYLVIA PLATH is the author of the poetry collections *The Colossus* (1960), *Ariel* (1965), *Crossing the Water: Transitional Poems* (1971), *Winter Trees* (1971), and *The Collected Poems* (1981). She also wrote *Three Women: A Monologue for Three Voices* (1962), *The Bell Jar* (1963), *Letters Home: Correspondence, 1950–1963* (1975), *Johnny Panic and the Bible of Dreams and Other Prose Writings* (1977), and *The Journals of Sylvia Plath* (1982).

LINDA GRAY SEXTON is the author of *Between Two Worlds: Young Women in Crisis* (1979), *Rituals* (1981), *Mirror Images* (1984), *Points of Light* (1988), *Private Acts* (1991), and *Searching for Mercy Street* (1994). In 1977, she edited *Anne Sexton: A Self-Portrait in Letters.*

LAUREN SLATER is the author of numerous short stories and essays and the memoirs *Welcome to My Country* (1996), *Prozac Diary* (1999), *Lying: A Metaphorical Memoir* (2001), and *Love Works Like This: Moving from One Kind of Life to Another* (2002).

TRACY THOMPSON is the author of *The Beast* (1995). She has worked as a newspaper reporter at *The Atlanta Constitution* and currently writes for *The Washington Post.*

MARY JANE WARD is the author of *The Tree Has Roots* (1937), *The Wax Apple* (1938), *The Snake Pit* (1946), *The Professor's Umbrella* (1948), *A Little Night Music* (1951), *It's Different for a Woman* (1952), *Counterclockwise* (1969), and *The Other Caroline* (1970).

PERMISSION CREDITS

ABOUT THE EDITOR

REBECCA SHANNONHOUSE is a freelance writer and editor. Her editorial credits include the Modern Library anthology *Under the Influence: The Literature of Addiction*. Her writing has appeared in *The New York Times,* the *San Francisco Chronicle, USA Today,* and other publications. She lives in Greenwich, Connecticut.

A NOTE ON THE TYPE

The principal text of this Modern Library edition
was set in a digitized version of Janson, a typeface that
dates from about 1690 and was cut by Nicholas Kis,
a Hungarian working in Amsterdam. The original matrices have
survived and are held by the Stempel foundry in Germany.
Hermann Zapf redesigned some of the weights and sizes for
Stempel, basing his revisions on the original design.

Printed in the United States
by Baker & Taylor Publisher Services